God of the Rahtid

God of the Rahtid

Redeeming Rage

Robert Beckford

DARTON · LONGMAN + TODD

First published in 2001 by
Darton, Longman and Todd Ltd
140–142 Wandsworth High Street
London SW18 4JJ

ISBN 0–232–52331–2

A catalogue record for this book is available from the British Library.

Designed by Sandie Boccacci
Phototypeset in 10/14pt Korinna by Intype London Ltd
Printed and bound in Great Britain by
Redwood Books, Trowbridge, Wiltshire

Contents

Preface

A multitude of conversations with Black friends over the last two years have caused me to reflect on rage, in particular how we Black people in Britain deal with or administer our rage. Black rage is complex and can not be covered in its entirety within this book. My concern is with a type of rage I witness and have experienced as a Black professional. I am particularly interested in the ways that African-Caribbean people who have 'made it' cope with the 'glass ceiling' imposed upon them despite their ability, expertise and experience. Many Black (African, African-Caribbean and Asian) people decide that the best way up the ladder is 'through the door' – leaving their post and establishing their own business – but many, in fact the majority, stay put and negotiate their resistance within their places of work, under surveillance, under pressure and – for many – growing increasingly vexed as a result of their experience of marginalisation or oppression.

However, there is also another source of Black rage that concerns me, outside of the workplace, in the world of representation – that is to say, the way in which Black people are represented in the media gets me angry, in a sort of 'low-level rage'. I spend a lot of time discussing images with students and friends as a sort of 'therapy' to reaffirm that being Black and male does not always mean being a sportsperson, singer, comedian, security officer or robber. Advertising agencies, television programmes, magazine editors and newspaper columnists still overlook Black diversity, complexity and creativity, in the way in which they represent Black people.

I believe that the task of theology is to make sense of the meaning of God in the world and, in my case, from the perspective of the Black community. This means being concerned with the real-life questions and concerns that arise from the community. An academic concern with meticulous, hair-splitting, intellectual questions – important as these may seem at times – cannot, therefore, be my theological starting point. Instead, as a second-generation African-Caribbean male in Britain from proletarian Jamaican stock, I make my starting point the life-setting of the majority of African-Caribbean people. In regard to Black rage, therefore, the question I must address is how we can make sense of these types of rage and redeem them, so that rage becomes a constructive force in our lives. In this book I have set out to show that Black theology offers an approach to the Bible and the Christian life that acknowledges and refocuses Black rage.

It is important to state at the outset that this book is concerned with Black rage in general and African-Caribbean rage in particular. I make this distinction because I am aware that there are issues relevant to all non-White people, but that there are also issues which differ amongst non-White people. Regarding the latter, I want to show how the rage felt by African-Caribbean people can be *redeemed* so that it becomes a constructive force in Black life. As a Black theologian concerned with the interface between Black religion and culture (religious-cultural analysis), it makes sense to examine what there is within my faith and cultural systems that provides (or does not provide) me with the resources to negotiate my rage. The results of my initial analysis are contained within this book.

God of The Rahtid is my third book concerned with developing ideas and resources for Christians concerned with racial justice in Britain. In *Jesus is Dread: Black Theology and Black Culture in Britain* (Darton, Longman and Todd, 1998) I identified resources and perspectives that Black theologians and the Black Church need to adopt in order to move from a *passive* to a *radical* orientation. In particular, I suggested that Black experience in Britain, Black culture and Black faith were essential resources for developing a Black theology that can speak prophetically to the socio-political and religious-cultural worlds in which Black people live. I developed a loose religious-cultural critical analysis where a dialogue between Black theology and Black cultural expression provided insights and perspectives for a Black liberation theology in Britain.

The interface between Black theology and Black cultural expression was further developed in *Dread and Pentecostal: A Political Theology for the Black Church in Britain* (SPCK, 2000), Here, I produced a framework for a Black political theology, which I termed Dread Pentecostal theology. Because Rastafari is the most significant liberation theology to emerge from Caribbean people in the last century, it made social, political and theological sense to appropriate aspects of Rastafari to challenge and reorientate aspects of Black faith in Britain to produce a liberative theology. In this case, by combining the Rastafarian concept of *dread* with aspects of Black Pentecostalism, I demonstrated how it is possible to 'conscientise' and politicise Black Pentecostalism.

In this third text my concern is to draw on the methodology developed in *Jesus is Dread* and *Dread Pentecostal Theology* to explore how Black faith, experience and socio-political analysis might assist Black people to redeem the rage that emerges from living under varied and complex systems of racialised oppression. *This is not intended to be a comprehensive, or global study, but instead, to provide insight into specific theological, personal and cultural issues that confront African-Caribbean people in Britain. It is an attempt to move towards a theological and cultural understanding of Black rage.*

In Chapter 1, 'Doing theology in the UKKK: towards a redemptive vengeance' (UK + KKK = racist Britain), I provide an analysis of the present situation, namely, how types of rage are experienced because of what I term *problematic inclusion* (representation in the media), and *pernicious exclusion* (the experience of racism). Through an exploration of the death of Diana, Princess of Wales, and the William Macpherson Report into the death of the Black teenager Stephen Lawrence, I suggest that one way in which Black theology can help in this area is to offer a redemption of rage, that is, a *redemptive vengeance*. Chapter 1 contours the socio-political dimensions of redemptive vengeance.

In Chapter 2, 'God of the rahtid', I explore the theological dimensions of redemptive vengeance. Here I suggest that developing an image of God as one who sides with those who have rage (or what I term *rahtid* – Jamaican derivative of 'wrath'), reconnects the righteousness of God with Black rage. The theological distance between God's righteousness and Black rage is bridged within the Kingdom of God. By drawing on the realised eschatologies within Black and womanist theologies, I show that the Kingdom of God provides a space where Black rage is redirected and refocused so that it becomes allied with God's quest for justice in the world today. Moreover, I will show that Black rage within the Kingdom of God has the potential to save not only Black people but also our oppressors. *In this book it is the former that is of central concern.* Having defined redemptive vengeance both socio-politically and theo-logically, this book then utilises redemptive vengeance as a heuristic to evaluate areas of Black existence where I suggest redemption must be explored. I begin with identity politics.

Chapters 3 and 4 explore how redemptive vengeance as a liberative paradigm can be explored in personal experience and cultural analysis respectively. Chapter 3, 'Name droppin'' is a personal story concerned with applying redemptive vengeance to identity politics, in particular, my attempt to redeem my Jam-aican slave name, 'Beckford'. If redemptive vengeance is to redeem it must begin with who I am and who we are as the African-Caribbean diaspora in Britain. Arguably the clearest example of racialised oppression in the personal sphere is the slave name, because in most cases it is synonymous with the English brutality and exploitation of Black people in the Caribbean. By applying redemptive vengeance to the history and politics of my slave name, I explore possible options available for redeeming the name as a way of resisting internalised racism.

In Chapter 4, 'Miseducation: Lauryn Hill and redemptive vengeance', I apply redemptive vengeance to Black expressive culture, in particular with an analysis of the award-winning debut album by hip-hop artist Lauryn Hill. My main concern here is to demonstrate how redemptive vengeance can be used as a paradigm to interrogate the redemptive qualities of hip-hop culture. Hip-hop is the most influential cultural tradition of the African diaspora in the last 25 years. After an analysis of the origins of hip-hop in the South Bronx, New York, I turn my attention to one of the most commercially successful and critically acclaimed rap albums of the latter part of the twentieth century, *The Miseducation of Lauryn Hill*. In short, I critique Hill's lyrics from the perspective of redemptive vengeance in order to challenge Hill's 'rebel' status.

In the final chapter, 'Redeeming the hustler', I take redemptive vengeance to one of the most tragic situations in Black Atlantic cultures ('Atlantic' is used to refer to the US and UK) – Black incarceration. As is the case in both the US and UK, Black people are over-represented in the criminal justice system. The reasons for this situation are addressed in brief, but the primary focus of this chapter is to describe a theological pedagogy for Black male prisoners which incorporates redemptive vengeance. In this chapter, I suggest that redemptive vengeance demands a rethinking of the locus of theological activity, theological pedagogy, and also theological texts. In sum I suggest that if Black theologians in particular and Black Christians in general wish to engage in the educational empowerment of the Black incarcerated, redemptive vengeance provides us with a framework for rethinking the form and content of Black theology.

The arguments, themes and perspectives of this book are the product of my theological imagination. Therefore, I take full responsibility for its contents. There are, however, several people who have assisted directly and indirectly. First, there are those who have provided insight into Black professional life, in particular Yvette Hutchinson and my sister Barbara Banda. Both of these brilliant and dedicated women have shown me what it means to struggle for justice 'inside Babylon'. Second, there are those who have continued to inspire me as a person and as a theologian. I am particularly grateful to my friend and colleague, Professor Randal Bailey, who visited me and gave me hope as I struggled to survive the pressures of academic life and assault on my ideas. Finally there are those who have supported me as I spent time at my desk. I am truly thankful to God for the efforts of my wife, Charlie, who has been my shield and staff as I have laboured with this book.

1.
Doing theology in the UKKK: towards a redemptive vengeance

Introduction: exploding categories: the Brixton bombing

The nail bomb attack in Brixton on Saturday 17 April 1999 was not a surprise to me. For decades Black communities in Britain have been victims of pernicious racial attacks. The death of Kelso Cochrane (1959), the New Cross Massacre (1980), the death of the teenager Stephen Lawrence (1993) and countless others all bear witness to the exploding categories of racialised violence.

In the aftermath of Brixton, some African-Caribbean Church leaders searched for theological resources in order to respond to the heightened reality of racial attacks on the Black community. They were searching because, despite fifty years of Black Churches in Britain, we have not yet developed explicit political theologies that unequivocally engage with the social policies and economic strategies that stalk Black communities. We have been too fearful of the consequences of upsetting the Establishment's 'apple cart'. The fear of the Black Church restricts its quest for a holistic or full gospel message. In her classic essay, 'The transformation of silence into language and action', the African American feminist Audre Lorde makes an intimate connection between fear, silence and wholeness:

the transformation of silence into language and action is

an act of self-revelation, and that always seems fraught
with danger . . . you're never really a whole person if you
remain silent, because there's always that one little piece
inside you that wants to be spoken out, and if you keep
ignoring it, it gets madder and madder and hotter and
hotter . . .[1]

Clear, articulate and measured Black theological perspectives,
no matter how diverse, are necessary especially when we consider the dangerous conditions under which Black people live in
Britain. If the Black Church does not have a voice (or voices)
on issues of racial justice, we will fail to support the 'least of
these' as commanded by Jesus in Matthew 25. Silence by the
Black Church is also problematic because there are numerous
campaigns and projects across the UK that are in need of
articulate and measured analysis and affirmation from Black
Christians.

However, it would be unfair to say that all Black Christians
have remained ignorant of the need for political engagement.
In recent years there has been an important development, in
particular, the launch of the Black Christian Civic Forum (BCCF)
in the winter of 1998. The BCCF reflects an effort by second-
and third-generation Black Christians to move the Church into
articulating a political theology. The BCCF political statement
reads:

The establishment of the Black Christian Civic Forum, UK
is a response by black Christians to the need for the
black-majority churches in Britain to get more involved in
politics and to speak clearly and prophetically on social
and racial justice issues.[2]

However, while allowance must be made for the fact that BCCF
is a relatively new organisation, so far what is not apparent is
what kind of political praxis undergirds it. Although BCCF has
representation on important government committees, it is also

important for it to create a grass-roots following by mobilising Church members. (Later I will show that there are issues of sexism that must also be addressed.)

I want to suggest some considerations for this new black theological politics. There is the need for *a new Black Church political practice based on old resources*. This issue will be tackled below. After that I will focus on the need for *a theology that takes seriously the rage induced by continued racialised oppression*.

1. New practice, old resources

What is required at the present time is a theological analysis that takes seriously the socio-political and religious-cultural concerns of Black people, all of which should lead to call *new practice*. Socio-political issues concern living out the Gospel in the concrete systems, structures and institutions in which we live. Religious-cultural issues are concerned with critical engagement with aspects of Black religion and culture. This is for the sake of identifying that which sustains and empowers Black people. In *Dread Pentecostal Theology* (SPCK, 2000) I refer to this gaze on Black life as a Dread Pentecostal theology. As a social theory, a *dread* gaze is concerned with contesting contemporary social relationships and challenging power relations both inside and outside of Christian communities. From a religious-cultural perspective, a dread gaze on Black faith is one that nurtures a healthy and critical engagement with all of life. A dread gaze also seeks wholeness both inside and outside of the Black community.

Dread Pentecostal theology is also concerned with practice, that is, the relationship between beliefs and actions. As Kathryn Tanner has illustrated in *The Politics of God*, Christian belief is a lived culture. Our actions and beliefs interact and inform each other on a daily basis. However, the relationship between beliefs and actions is complex and not always a clear-cut equation.[3] In the case of African-Caribbean Christianity in Britain, the first generation tended to combine beliefs on justice in the world with an otherworldly eschatology (theology of the end times). As a result, our quest for justice in this world has been muted by the belief that 'Jesus is coming soon'. For the adherents of this tradition, therefore, any meaningful participation in this world becomes a waste of 'precious prayer time'.

In recent years, some second- and third-generation Christians and churches have come to believe that justice and material blessing go together – that is, God's justice is experienced here in increased material blessing. The outcome is the upsurge in 'prosperity' doctrines. Both of these theological responses fail to interrogate the structural issues within the contemporary context. For those of us in the academy there is a challenge to provide a theology of change that addresses and challenges our churches to deal effectively with an analysis that struggles with the events, concerns and issues of the day. Although Manning Marable is speaking about social theory, Black theologians in Britain should pay attention to his advice to Black activists in America: 'To be liberating, any social theory must reflect the actual problems of an historical conjuncture with a commitment to rigor and scholastic truth.'[4]

The need for a liberating theology was the motivation behind the Bible and Racial Attacks Conference in February 1999. I wanted to reflect theologically on the upsurge in racial violence. I wanted to ask questions such as, 'What does God have to say to a community living with the threat of nail bombs from Neo-Nazi organisations?' 'Does the Bible assist us in making sense of and finding a positive response to the situation?' And, 'How do we mobilise the Black Church to respond effectively to the new situation?' With my colleague Yvette Hutchinson, and with support from the Bible Society, we organised the Bible and Racial Attacks Conference. This conference brought together Church members, community workers and theologians from the

African diaspora. Our aim was to marry theological analysis with social action as a response to racial attacks. The conference was both inter-disciplinary and inter-faith; we wanted to explore how we could stand in solidarity with other faith communities. The outcome was not only the production of papers and recommendations but also renewed alliances between social activists, Black nationalists and Black theologians. Furthermore, it became increasingly clear through our historical analysis that resources for a theology of social change exist within Black Church history, specifically the history of Pentecostalism. This leads to my second resource for the new Black Christian politics in Britain, that is, *old resources.*

The roots of Pentecostalism provide us with important paradigms for Black and radical political theologies today. The Black political roots of Pentecostalism have been watered down. As Walter Hollenweger argues, while many contemporary charismatic and evangelical Churches have their roots in the origins of Pentecostalism, most have divorced themselves from the social justice at the heart of the origins of Pentecostalism.[5] Similarly, many Black Pentecostals are simply unaware of the sociopolitical motivations that produced their Christian tradition. I want to revisit the origins of Pentecostalism to show that we can discover models for combining belief with the quest for social justice. There are three areas of importance; *glossolalia, Christian practice* and *culture.*

Although others had focused on the role of glossolalia (speaking in tongues) as the initial sign of being filled with the Spirit,[6] it was the Black minister William Seymour (1870–1922) who linked glossolalia with social transformation. A generation before the Civil Rights Movement and Dr Martin Luther King, Seymour realised that one's commitment to the Gospel of Christ could not result in oppressive practices towards one's fellow men and women. He developed a theological praxis in and through glossolalia.

For the Azusa Church the gift of speaking in tongues was

not just an initial sign of receiving the Holy Spirit, but also a signifier of a commitment to radical social transformation.[7] The gift of tongues was a continuation of a just world order established by God in the New Testament Church. Therefore, the outpouring of tongues in the small church on Azusa Street in 1906 was a continuation of this order.[8] Therefore, one could *not* have tongues and continue with forms of social discrimination. In other words, what we witness here is the birth of a political pneumatology. That is to say, the Azusa revival teaches us that the Spirit of God is a force for challenging discriminatory social structures in the world today. In this sense, as Michael Dyson has suggested, speaking in tongues can be experienced as speaking a radical language of equality.[9]

The connection between tongues and the social world has been lost as Pentecostalism spread beyond Azusa. However, as Alan Anderson has argued in the South African context, in some cases the relationship between pneumatology, power and radical social change remained.[10] One way in which we might revive the political potentiality of Pentecostal pneumatology is by re-contextualising the interpretation of tongues so that it is reconnected in a more explicit way to social change. One dimension of the gift of interpretation, from the perspective of political pneumatology, is the ability to carry over the language of the Spirit-equality into the concrete world where colour, gender, wealth and sexual orientation restrict and limit life opportunities. If every Black Pentecostal Church in Britain viewed tongues as a language of social engagement rather than just a supra-rational ecstatic experience, what spiritual power would be unleashed in Britain's urban centres!

A second theme in the birth of Pentecostalism that is of importance is the anti-oppressive Christian praxis that emerged from the doctrine of glossolalia. Despite the highly segregated societies across the West Coast of North America at the start of the twentieth century, Seymour's Church developed an anti-racist, anti-sexist and anti-classist ministry. Even the seating arrangement embodies this egalitarian theme:

> Worshippers gathered in a new way completely equal in the house of God, the body of Christ not a collection of individuals looking over the back of many heads simply to the clergy or choir but an intimate whole serving one another. This unconventional seating plan revealed Seymour's conviction that events transpiring at Azusa Mission were different, unique and revolutionary.[11]

Ithiel Clemmons is correct when he argues that the Azusa Street Church represented a 'true koinonia'.[12] In *Dread and Pentecostal*, I demonstrated how the political pneumatology of Azusa was a *dread* happening, a 'kairos' moment of freedom, empowerment and liberation. In short, the combination of dread and Azusa's pneumatology creates a *dread pneumatology* concerned with the Spirit's participation in the struggle for justice.[13]

The final theme that is a resource for social justice emerging from Azusa is culture. Seymour utilised Black cultural resources in order to develop a holistic ministry at Azusa. His use of Black culture was twofold. On the one hand, the dominant social and Church cultural practices needed to be challenged. The cultural practices and social milieu of Azusa needed to reflect the new sense of freedom, power and love experienced through the out-pouring of the Spirit. On the other hand, Seymour demonstrated that aspects of Black culture could be mobilised in the quest for wholeness. For example, the early movement made use of the Black music tradition. Walter Hollenweger states: 'He [Seymour] affirmed his Black heritage by introducing Negro spirituals and Negro music into his liturgy at a time when this music was considered inferior and unfit for Christian worship.'[14]

However, Seymour's cultural contribution was more than the introduction of music. As MacRobert demonstrates, Seymour brought to Azusa the Black religious heritage. This was a religious tradition that utilised story, song, dance, poly-rhythmic clapping and the swaying of bodies.[15] What is important here is the recognition that Christian religion is a cultural system.[16] Therefore, 'to have Church' is also to experience and explore culture. Seymour demonstrates one way in which we can redeem Black cultural forms so that they become vehicles for interpreting Black faith. His life and experience reveal how it is possible to develop a personal orientation that enables the Black 'self' to respond positively to negative surroundings. This leads to the central concern of this chapter, Black rage.

2. Analysing Black rage

As mentioned above, as well as the need for *a new Black Church political practice based on old resources*, there is also a need for *a theology that takes seriously the rage induced by continued racialised oppression.* Since I sat down to write *Jesus is Dread* in the summer of 1997, much has happened. We have witnessed the rise in explicit and violent forms of racism. We have also witnessed the emergence of a small group of Black Church activists dedicated to 'dragging' Black Churches into the world of politics. However, what concerns me most is the issue of Black rage. This is because Black rage remains an area of analysis underexamined in African-Caribbean diasporan thought. Likewise, while the Black Church has provided a cathartic outlet for Black rage, it has not developed a coherent theology to address this matter.

Black rage is a complex phenomenon comprising external and internal manifestations. Internalised rage can lead to physical and psychological manifestations, usually physical and mental illness. Externalised rage can take on a variety of forms including the collective rage that is witnessed in social protest and uprisings. The causes of rage are complex, but I want to focus here on what I call *low level rage*. Low-level rage is related to internalised rage in that it is experienced in mind and body.

It is manifest in anger, depression and anxiety. Many Black people experience this kind of rage every day by virtue of living in what bell hooks calls 'a white supremacist, capitalist society'.[17] One of the failings of my previous writings was my inability to explore the rage that is a direct result of the low-level depression and anxiety which stalks many of us as we live out our lives in neo-colonial Britain. According to the Black psychiatrist Dr Fred Hickling, low-level rage is more widespread and more dangerous to Black people than we would care to think. As a result, *low-level rage must be tackled in any quest for individual or communal wholeness.*[18] I want to outline at least two causes of low-level rage that are relevant to this study.

First, rage caused by *problematic inclusion.* This rage is related to *representation,* that is, it is generated by the ways in which Black people are represented within society. Because of the negative and unsophisticated ways in which we are positioned and represented, a few evenings of watching television or reading the press can be an uncomfortable experience for Black people who are socially and politically aware of the contemporary context. Likewise, examining the statistics of major institutions such as those concerned with education or the criminal justice system can be a depressing experience when one locates and examines the positions of Black people within these spaces. Second, there is a rage caused by *pernicious exclusion.* This rage is related to social exclusion and discrimination. It is the rage generated by inequality. For example, the racist attacks that caused the deaths of Stephen Lawrence and Michael Menson are events that evoke low-level rage because they bear witness to the ways Black people are denied equal treatment before the law. Theologically speaking, *problematic inclusion* and *pernicious exclusion* define Black people as less than and therefore not fully part of God's creation.

Low-level rage must be redeemed in the struggle for Black wholeness, and identifying the workings of problematic inclusion and pernicious exclusion is central to redeeming Black rage. To this end, that of *redeeming rage*, I want to demonstrate how these forms of low-level rage can be articulated and understood through an evaluation of two recent events. These were the death of Diana, Princess of Wales, and the Macpherson Report into the death of the Black teenager, Stephen Lawrence.

The death of Diana

As mentioned above, low-level rage can be caused by problematic inclusion. Below I want to outline how this rage became evident for me as I watched the events unfold around the death of Diana, Princess of Wales.

For days, in the summer of 1997, like many other African and African-Caribbean people, I watched the TV, conversed with friends, and followed arguments in the press and on the Internet. The subject was the death of Diana, Princess of Wales. As I consumed the events, information and discussions, I was amazed at the dramatic increase in the presence and inclusion of Black British people in television and radio reports. In comparison, only a few months earlier, during the general election, Black opinions and issues had been avoided by astute election spin-doctors and political advisers, who predicted that issues of race, from either the 'right' or 'left', were a vote-loser. But after the death of Diana, Black presence, opinions and presentation were *en vogue*.

As I observed this multiculturalism, two questions formed at the forefront of my mind. First, 'Why and how are Black people being positioned in the ways that we are?' And second, 'What does our inclusion mean as part of a broader religious and cultural analysis?'

Why and how are Black people being positioned in the ways that we are?

The first question concerns the motivations of Black people and of the media.

Black people's motivations

Regarding Black people's motivations, deconstructing our responses is important because how we respond, according to Frantz Fanon, is part of a process of 'Self-recognition in relation to the White Other'.[19] That is, self-recognition is about how we place ourselves in relation to the State, British society and our local communities. Since our arrival in the 'new world', diasporan Africans, displaced and dislocated from our origins, have engaged in a self-representational 'play' in order to resist and survive.[20] Regarding the motivations behind Black responses to Diana's death, there were those who chose not to express any concern over it and got on with their lives despite the mass hysteria taking place. However, there were those who chose to represent themselves in particular ways and there are three areas that I would like to outline. These are *grief, signifying*, and *conspiracy*.

Grief concerns the authentic outpouring of emotion expressed by African-Caribbean people over this event. Grief, in this context, was not an attempt to signify (even though on one level everything signifies) in a conscious way. It was 'real' in the sense that it was a genuine and honest response. Arguably the most striking image was a Black man in tears outside the gates of Buckingham Palace, crying, distraught and falling to his knees from the weight of his distress. His image circulated globally in television and newspaper images of grief. Such was the quality of his display that a friend of mine thought he might have been a professional mourner! For some, grief was related to empathy. African-Caribbean people identified with Diana's personal struggle, and her charitable concerns; her loss was also their loss. Further, within most African-Caribbean cultures public spontaneous outpourings of grief are a natural part of our emotional repertoire, although the ratio of public to private grief differs in every cultural situation.[21] Hence it was not unusual to see African-Caribbean people expressing grief. (As we shall see later, the media appropriated African-Caribbean grief as an authenticating symbol.) Another aspect of African-Caribbean grief is action. When something bad happens, our cultural framework propels us into action. As a good friend says, 'When death occurs, we fry fish and dumplin' and go visit the dead house.' In this case, Buckingham Palace was out of bounds. But exclusion of the public from the Palace itself did not prevent a number of African-Caribbean people being some of the first to lay flowers and stand outside the Palace early in the morning after the car crash.

In opposition to grief is *signifying*. Signifying concerns the ways in which African-Caribbean cultures 'play', 'manoeuvre' and 'conjure' a subject, issue or event so as to arrive at 'direction through indirection'.[22] Signifying can be a form of 'trickery' that enables oppressed people to negotiate or manipulate the dominant power. When this Anancification[23] (signifying on life as found in the stories of Anancy the spider in Caribbean folk culture) is applied to the death of Diana it suggests that, for some, a display of sympathy was a veneer. The death of Diana created a space for some of us to 'signify' on cultural allegiance. That is, African-Caribbean distress was a construction, a form of signifying on the demands for a show of loyalty from the Black community. However, for some of us, signifying was necessary because of media pressure. For example, Central News and BBC Midlands were keen to show in news reports how Black people were responding. Hence, a lot of Black and Asian people felt pressured. We had to show that we were just as concerned as everybody else was. So we put on our masks and played the part.

The problem with signifying is that it comes with a psychological price. Suppressing one's real thoughts, ideas and beliefs in order to conform are not good for self-image or self-actualisation. For far too long many of us within the African diaspora have lived and played out this schizophrenic existence at personal cost. I am convinced that many Black people in psychiatric hospitals are there because they have refused, forgotten or lost the ability to 'fit in' or be 'assimilated' due to the stresses of signifying.

The final area concerned with African-Caribbean motivation is *conspiracy*. Conspiracy refers to the way in which African-Caribbean people sought to identify more sinister motives and reasons behind Diana's death. At one end of the spectrum there were clusters of conspiracy theories relating to Diana's possible marriage to a brown-skinned Muslim. This school argued that the British State would not allow a non-White person entry into the royal clan. They argued for British secret service involvement with her death. The sociological construction of conspiracy is predicated on the 'glass ceiling' complex. This is the belief that African-Caribbean people will always be excluded from the highest echelons of society. At the other end of the conspiracy spectrum were clusters of rumours. These rumours lacked the intellectual sophistication of conspiracy theories but were just as effective in the production of doubt. This second school argued that Diana's death was inevitable because she had sought to be different and, in so doing, challenged the State. This sociological construction of rumour is predicated upon the 'good-die-young' complex.[24]

Grief, signifying and *conspiracy* reveal the ways in which Black people chose to represent ourselves in and through the death of Diana. What these motivations suggest is that some of us viewed ourselves as integrally linked to what was taking place and others did not. However, what is significant for me is that much of what took place amongst Black people was in response to pressure to go along with the 'hype'. To this end, many colluded indirectly with the press hysteria over the cross-cultural significance of the Princess of Wales only weeks after being ignored by the press during the general election. What was even more problematic was the way in which the press chose to reconfigure these Black motivations. This leads to the second part of the first question, 'Why and *how* are Black people being positioned in the ways that we are?'

The media

This part of the question is about media politics. I am concerned with the ways in which Black people are represented in the White-dominated press. Numerous Black cultural critics and sociologists have demonstrated how the positioning of African-Caribbean and other Black peoples in Britain signifies a plethora of political, social and ideological battles in post-colonial Britain. I am interested in what Theophus Smith calls the pharmacopoeia – the ability of cultural forms to heal or to harm.[25]

There are two issues that concern the representation of African-Caribbean people in the media. These can be summarised under two headings: (1) *authenticating* and (2) *demonising Blackness*.

Authenticating Blackness[26] is a reversal of authenticating Whiteness. In short, it is the cultural process by which African-Caribbean cultural signatures are introduced into a cultural context or social reality for the purpose of adding value or credibility. Authenticating Blackness occurs at various levels in popular culture but is most clearly witnessed in music. For example, the inclusion of Black singers in the pop groups The Spice Girls, All Saints, S Club 7 and Another Level are examples of authenticating Blackness; similar is the the use of Black dancers/singers by Mariah Carey and George Michael. Turning to the death of Diana, authenticating Blackness occurred in numerous locations.

First there was the use of African-Caribbean grief to add

value and credibility to the tragedy. There was an over-representation of African-Caribbean people grieving both in newsprint and television. African-Caribbean people became authenticating symbols of Diana's universal appeal. For example, many commentators spoke of the 'multiracial scenes' at the 'open-air shrines' at Buckingham and Kensington Palaces and also in the crowd on the day of the funeral. Second, African and African-Caribbean spiritual leaders were introduced to authenticate Diana's appeal to the marginalised. For example, on the day of her funeral two Black Anglican bishops, John Sentamu and Wilfred Wood, gave interviews on a national radio station, Radio 5. Normally it takes an explicitly Black concern for Radio 5 to speak to an African or African-Caribbean bishop. In this case, Radio 5's mobilisation of African-Caribbean representatives bespeaks authentication.

The second theme, *demonising Blackness*, refers to the negative association of Black people with the tragic. From Graeco-Roman times to the present, Blackness has been seen as a signifier of death in the European imagination. In some cases European literary culture introduces an African person (sometimes Ethiopian) to mark the point of death of a noble European.[27] European colour symbolism typifies Blackness as a signifier of death and mourning. Furthermore, in the wake of Diana's death, African-Caribbean people were portrayed as grieving in a highly emotional way. Hence, an extra dimension was added to this construct, that of Blackness as uncontrolled emotionalism. The over-representation of African-Caribbean peoples also continues an association of Blackness as authenticating the tragic and 'untamed' emotionalism surrounding Diana's death, thereby maintaining negative images of Black people in some White psyches.

In concluding my answer to the first question, I want to suggest that despite the varied ways in which Black people chose to represent themselves, the press chose more problematic images which, while attempting to assimilate Black images into the unfolding story, did so in a negative way. Hence, the death of Diana provides us with an example of problematic inclusion. I turn now to the second question.

What does our inclusion mean as part of a broader religious and cultural analysis?

The second question at the forefront of my mind was about the meaning of Black representation when placed within a broader religious cultural analysis. In short, how might I read these events as a Black theologian concerned with religious-cultural analysis, particularly the interface between media representation and theology? From my perspective, the press representation of Black motives produced a fictitious relationship between Diana and the Black community, which can be illustrated in three religious-cultural images of Diana.

Diana as patron saint of the Black oppressed

The first image that I witnessed within the Diana death narrative was Diana as patron saint of the Black oppressed. This image arises out of the ways in which grief was manipulated by the media. Diana was presented as a saviour figure for all Black people. This does not mean that there were not Black people who felt strongly about her. For example, in one African-Caribbean Methodist church in Birmingham, an African-Caribbean Church member put a picture of Diana on the altar during a Sunday morning service. This suggested to me that for some Black people Diana had been elevated in death to the ancestors in the African-Caribbean pantheon. On the one hand such appropriation represents a great ability amongst some Black people to love the monarch while possibly being sceptical about the State. As Richard Burton has shown, the Good monarch/ Bad State dialectic runs deep in Caribbean history.[28]

On the other hand there are some critical issues that emerge from this image. First, is Diana worthy of African-Caribbean beatification? For example, in comparison to other royal or non-royal people she has done very little to challenge racism, empower African-Caribbean youth or assist African-Caribbean enterprise. Second, her elevation is problematic when read through the eyes of womanist Christology.[29] Jacquelyn Grant has encouraged African-Caribbean people to see the 'Jesus of Faith' in the faces of African-Caribbean women who have characterised Christ's quest for liberation. In comparison, Diana's elevation at best weakens and at worst ignores the witness/contribution of African-Caribbean women who have struggled for African-Caribbean liberation. In sum, Diana's elevation might also be read as a domestic neo-colonial gesture – that is, we still prefer White saints to watch over us because we are not sure if the African or African-Caribbean ones can really help us.

Diana as surrogate Black Madonna

The second image that emerges from the media's handling of Diana's death is that of Diana as surrogate Black Madonna. This image is related to her involvement in the banning of land mines. Constant reference to this campaign during her death narratives presented Diana in a maternal relationship to needy African people. On occasion these images placed Black people as co-workers in a struggle against injustice. However, in the main, the images of Diana holding African babies in Africa re-created old colonial images of African dependency. In short, the image of Diana as a surrogate Black mother implies that benevolent White women have suckled African-Caribbean babies. As the converse is a literal fact, this role-reversal consigns the nurture by African-Caribbean women of White babies from the pages of history to myth.[30] Moreover, this image subverts the importance of African-Caribbean Madonnas and their theological, historical and spiritual significance.[31] Black

Madonnas in Western European thought represent an image, rare in the European imagination, of African people as sacred.

Queen of (Black) hearts

The third image that arises out of the aftermath of Diana's death is that of the 'Queen of (Black) hearts'. This image is seen in the authenticating grief motif outlined above. In short, the grief displayed by African-Caribbean people implies a high regard in African-Caribbean lives and hearts. It was Diana herself who used the phrase 'Queen of hearts' to symbolise her affinity with the people. But what does this appropriation mean from a Black Christian political perspective?[32]

First, the heart, in African-Caribbean Pentecostal thought, is very important. It is understood as the seat of consciousness and divine space. Therefore, whatever is put in the heart is a crucial statement about allegiance. This is why African-Caribbean Pentecostals take seriously Jesus' warning that what is in the heart will bear fruit in one's life: 'A good man (*sic*) out of the good treasure of the heart bringeth forth good things: and an evil man out of the evil treasure bringeth forth evil things' (Matthew 12:35).

The idea of Diana as the Queen of Black hearts is not impossible, or without benefit. As mentioned above, Black people have revealed that it is possible to transcend racialised boundaries and embrace the 'Other'. However, such a gesture has difficulties. In contexts where Black women of virtue have been hidden from history, the preoccupation with a White one ignores the African-Caribbean 'Queens'. In sum, don't the Black women who have played an important role in Black survival in the past and present have a close (if not un-critical) affinity with the aspirations and sensibilities of Black people in Britain? Don't they deserve pride of place in African-Caribbean hearts?

In sum, despite their limited benefit, all of the images which emerge from a broader religious-cultural analysis of the death of Diana represent problematic inclusion. For me, as mentioned above, constant exposure to problematic inclusion generates a sense of exasperation and the kind of low-level rage outlined above.

The death of Stephen Lawrence

The second major event that has taken place since writing *Jesus is Dread* was the enquiry into the death of the murdered Black teenager, Stephen Lawrence. His racist murder in April 1993 and the subsequent campaign to find his racist murderers was a landmark in British race relations. The campaign revealed the incompetence of the police, particularly how their racial profiling led to the suspected murderers getting away. In short, the events surrounding Stephen's death made the public aware of what Black people had been saying for over forty years – racism in the police force is endemic. The campaign to find Stephen's killers culminated in a public inquiry in 1999. The Macpherson Report contained the inquiry's findings.

The Macpherson Report made several ground-breaking recommendations, including making the police and other government institutions subject to the Race Relations Act. In short, the police are now under the same scrutiny as the private sector in regard to racist practice.

As in the case of the death of Diana, my concern was with what implications the events would have for the Black community. After the death of Stephen, there were a multitude of religious-cultural images that arose from the media reporting of the case. Two are worth noting. First, there were the 'noble savage' representations of Doreen and Neville Lawrence in the press (dignified, responsible and hard-working Black folk). Second, their portrayal in heroic terms in posters and paintings, as a couple who combined professional aspirations and determination with non-subversiveness, was also deeply culturally significant. However, I was particularly interested in how the Macpherson Report would challenge churches, because a central and most controversial aspect of the report was the description and application of 'institutionalised racism'. The report describes institutionalised racism as:

> the collective failure of an organisation to provide an appropriate and professional service to people because of their colour, culture, or ethnic origin. It can be seen or detected in processes, attitudes and behaviour which amount to discrimination through unwitting prejudice, ignorance, thoughtlessness and racist stereotyping which disadvantage minority ethnic people.[33]

As mentioned earlier, I am concerned with problematic inclusion and pernicious exclusion. The latter provokes the rage that is related to social exclusion and discrimination. *It is the rage generated by inequality.* In this second section, I want to explore pernicious exclusion and, as in the case above, to provide a religious focus for my analysis. In this case I will explore pernicious exclusion by first evaluating the White Church in Britain in response to the description of 'institutionalised racism'. I do this because this area of application of Macpherson has not been subject to public analysis. However, what I also want to show is that, as was the case with *problematic inclusion*, in terms of *pernicious exclusion* Black people must also consider how it is that we directly or indirectly *collude* with this form of racialised oppression.

Macpherson and the White Church

White Christianity has been a central legitimising force behind the colonial and imperial subjugation of Black people. Put more clearly, within the African-Caribbean tradition, despite his sexist language, Marcus Garvey was most articulate in identifying the cultural reality that stands behind every theological system when he said: 'If the White man has the idea of a White God, let him worship his God as he desires . . .'[34] In the latter part of the twentieth century, reflecting British society's racist tendencies, the White Church and European theology has played a role in the development of cultural racism(s). Cultural racisms target cultural traditions as the central arena for exclusion. Take, for example, how a particular type of White, patriarchal Englishness dominates the local and national Methodist, Anglican and URC Churches.

For a long time those who spoke about racism and the White Church were viewed as 'trouble-makers', or lacking 'the Spirit of reconciliation'. However, today the critique of Whiteness within English Christianity comes from the highest levels: 'The organisational culture of the Church of England . . . is still socially glued together by a culture that is monochrome – that is White . . . it still lacks colour and spice.' Bishop John Sentamu's statement to Synod in July of 1999 corresponded in part to Foucault's critical analysis of power.[35] That is, the norm – the privileging of White skin colour in theology – has to demean all systems and ideas that challenge its supremacy. Hence, Sentamu continues, 'the expectation of the historic, White, educated, elite English norm is maintained, regardless of the make up of a congregation.'

As suggested above in the quotation from Garvey, one consequence of a Church that has a monochrome culture is the production of a theology that reflects its cultural politics. In other words, the theology of Anglicanism and other English denominations supports the maintenance of the White male hierarchy. What I want to identify here is White liberal Christianity's flirtation with the *theological politics of evasion*.

Theological politics of evasion

The privileging of White skin colour in theological circles is witnessed in the theological politics of evasion. There are three types of argument.

First, 'race' is simply omitted from theological discourse. This is why it is possible, in the midst of racial murders, attacks, unfair prosecutions, Black unemployment and underemployment, for most White theologians, even those concerned with a social or cultural agenda, to ignore, sidestep or devalue racial politics in Britain. A useful example is Deborah Sawyer and Diane Collier's *Is There a Future for Feminist Theology?* (Sheffield Academic Press, 1999). This text explores feminist theology, primarily in the UK although there is some reference to the US. What is most intriguing from the perspective of the theological politics of evasion is the ignoring of womanist perspectives. It is clear that these White women did not listen to Hazel Carby![36]

The limited theological challenge within academic circles enables popular White theology to make the same evasive manoeuvre. Take for example, Mark Wallinger's *Ecce Homo* – the sculpture of Jesus installed in July 1999 in Trafalgar Square, London. Wallinger's Jesus, symbolising his view of Christ's humanity, is White, English and male. The image wrestles Jesus' iconography away from the grandiose images of empire and places him amongst the ordinary [White] folk of the land. On the negative side, it is a recontextualisation (still a million miles away from multicultural London) which is characterised by the cross-cultural influences from Asia and the Caribbean that have resulted in highly syncretised urban cultures in England. An opportunity was missed to represent the Christ of faith as one who speaks and relates to a multicultural society. Similarly, it is also a recontextualisation several times removed from the historical Jesus, a first-century Jew and man of colour. As a consequence Wallinger reaffirms some of the psychosocial themes inherent in the Aryan images of Jesus that adorn most British chapels, church halls and stained-glass windows. Is this what Macpherson means by institutionalised racism being 'unwitting'?

The second aspect of the theological politics of evasion concerns the ways that White theologians seek to blame Black people equally with Whites for the state of the nation's racism. According to White radicals this type of reasoning occurs in White liberal society when Black folks have left the room! The theological rationale at work is based on the application of the belief that 'all have sinned and come short of the glory of God'. Therefore, Black people have in some ways contributed to the dangerous racial climate, be it through strife, envy or apathy. Because all sin is equal in its abhorrence to God (sin is sin), Black people cannot claim any moral high ground on matters of racialised oppression. On this platform the theological politics of evasion points to examples of Black passivity or apathy, which affect Whites adversely, as examples of areas of life where Black people contribute to a negative racial climate. However, this claim of equivalency between Black and White is based on fatal flaws.

While it would be ludicrous to deny any culpability on the part of Black people, it is fair to say that there is no equality between Black and White blameworthiness in racialised politics in contemporary Britain. One only needs to examine statistics on mental health, employment or immigration to see who has real power to oppress in this relationship. Likewise, one can read report after report on the racism in housing, the criminal justice system, education or attacks on individuals, to discover the negative bias that affects the quality and nature of life Black people can expect in Britain. Second, this reasoning fails to evaluate the history of inequality shaped in slavery and colonialism. This appeal to the past is not some crude attempt to negate any evidence of Black collusion or blame for the present difficulties. Instead, I want to remind those who occupy this ground that racism in Britain today is the product of limits and disadvantage placed on Black life in the long histories of slavery, colonialism and 1950s domestic neo-colonialism in the UK. We have not had the same starting points or positions of power in the discussion and evaluation of racism. The Macpherson Report encourages White liberal Christianity to come clean: acknowledge its racism and join in the struggle for racial justice.

Macpherson and the Black Church

As mentioned above, the Macpherson Report also has implications for the Black Church in Britain. In particular there are areas where it challenges some of the ways in which Black Churches directly or indirectly collude with pernicious exclusion. There are two areas of collusion which I want to discuss under the banner of *internalised pernicious exclusion*. These are *selfish* and *selfless faith*.

Colluding with pernicious exclusion

In response to Macpherson, the Black Church must also do some soul-searching. The Macpherson inquiry was responsible for conscientising many Black churches. A few Churches participated in the campaign, hosted conferences and developed strategies for dealing with racism and racist attack, and began to take seriously the need to find political tools to address racism. Interestingly, the representation of Stephen's parents as noble, dignified and honourable meant that even the Black Christians had to take note! For example, as mentioned above, the formation of the Black Christian Civic Forum represents this trend. While the BCCF represents an important starting point, it will need to take seriously internalised pernicious exclusion in its organisational structure. Upon the launch of the new organisation, the *Voice* newspaper stated:

> The recently launched Black Christian Civic Forum which aims to champion political justice issues concerning the

Black community, has appointed its executive body. Members comprise chairman Dr. Friday Nwator, general secretary Abraham Lawrence and Geoffrey Brandt as treasurer. Davey Johnson and Ron Nathen serve as executive members. David Muir the founder of the BCCF, will be executive director.[37]

The lack of female representation within the first executive of the Black Christian Civic Forum is problematic. Without gender equality, the BCCF is severely limited in its appeal and support. This is not a new situation in Black Atlantic politics. Within the complex history of the Civil Rights Movement gender concerns were suppressed in order for the challenge of racism to be predominant. In order not to duplicate the forms of structural oppression identified by Macpherson, the Black Church must examine its own 'house' in order not to collude with injustice by manifesting sexist practice.

The BCCF represents a rare excursion from the norm. One trend of Black Church life today (unlike Black Christianity in the nineteenth century), is to neglect explicit political involvement, opting instead for a crude mix of otherworldly spirituality and this-worldly materialism through problematic prosperity doctrines that lead into what I want to call a *selfish faith* rather than a *selfless faith*.

The Bible describes a *selfish faith* that is primarily concerned with the individual. The classic example of selfish faith in Scripture is when the disciples argue about who will be greatest in the Kingdom of heaven. Matthew 18:1–4 reads:

At the same time came the disciples unto Jesus, saying, who is the greatest in the kingdom of heaven? And Jesus called a little child unto him, and set him in the midst of them, And said, Verily I say unto you, Except ye be converted, and become as little children, ye shall not enter into the kingdom of heaven. Whosoever therefore shall humble himself as this little child, the same is greatest in the kingdom of heaven.

Selfish faith is self-seeking, self-demanding and self-rewarding. It is less concerned with the community or with the world, and more concerned with self-gain. In many Black Churches in Britain, we are entering a period where a selfish faith is easy to profess because it does not cost anything – it is only concerned with the personal. Some may wonder if a kind of faith that is solely concerned with the individual can be real faith at all! The common interest for those with selfish faith is 'Bless me, Lord'. Selfish faith is unable to answer the pressing social problems confronting the Black community. This is because selfish faith allows its adherents to be convinced that material blessing is the result of their hard work and faithfulness to God. Conversely, the plight of the poor, homeless or outcast is a result of their own wrongdoings. What I want to suggest is that, as was the case with the gender politics within BCCF, the Macpherson Report challenges selfish faith and encourages the Black Church to look outward and be concerned instead with a selfless faith.

Selfless faith is outward looking: it is concerned with faith in the world. It seeks to focus the power of God on transforming the world in which we live. It sees the mission and purpose of the Church as meaningless if it does not go beyond the physical boundaries of the church. Selfless faith is also prophetic: it seeks to show what is possible, not what is *im*possible, in the world today. It nurtures a spirituality that is geared towards empowering all, including the 'least of these', in the locality. Its hallmark is found in the practice of giving and not expecting anything in return. Selfless faith is not easy to profess because it is costly: it will cost everything – it will even cost our lives!

Above, I have attempted to show that *problematic inclusion* and *pernicious exclusion* are forces that fuel what I have termed low-level Black rage in Britain. In sum, I have suggested that in a post-literate visual world, the way in which Black people are represented can be a cause of outrage and low-level rage. Moreover, we still see the undisguised and shameless face of racism in exclusionary practices inside and outside of the Church. I have not claimed, however, that Black people are altogether free from some responsibility for the causes of our distress; instead, on occasion we have colluded with the forces of oppression.

In the final section of this introduction, I want to outline a way ahead for those concerned with exterminating problematic inclusion and pernicious exclusion, that is, a framework for dealing with the low-level rage I have identified above. This new system I call *redemptive vengeance*.

3. Towards redemptive vengeance

For me, the defining events mentioned above reveal the continued difficulties stalking Black people in Britain. We now live in an historical period marked by increased depression and anxiety over the safety and level of justice we can expect in racialised Britain. Given the danger of low-level rage and anxiety evident at the beginning of the new millennium, I suggest that the future of Black theology in Britain must be to develop theologies that embrace and redeem Black rage.

By definition, redemptive vengeance is concerned with the constructive use of Black rage. As shown above, there are numerous occasions where Black rage is justified and necessary. In such cases our principled anger must have an outlet. To ensure that this righteous anger or vengeance is used to its best effects, it must be redemptive. To be redemptive, 'vengeance' must seek more than Black freedom – it must provide an avenue for total transformation of the situation. Total transformation means changing the lives of the oppressed and oppressors so that the sins that cause division are eliminated. For me this is what is meant by *love* – total transformation based on renewal. The kind of framework I am proposing has boundaries. This will become clearer in Chapter 2, when I compare redemptive vengeance with compensatory and punitive vengeance.

Redemptive vengeance is not new in African-Caribbean or Black Atlantic history. Most attempts to utilise righteous anger in a redemptive manner constitute redemptive vengeance. This means that redemptive vengeance has not been the sole property of Black Christians. For example, the late Malcolm X, who had moved to a greater understanding of Islam, ethnicity and racial politics, exemplified a non-Christian example of redemptive vengeance.[38] Similarly *aspects* of Nelson Mandela's presidency in South Africa might also be considered examples of redemptive vengeance. Mandela encouraged Blacks to focus their rage into acts of reconciliation. Despite the limited redistribution of wealth and the one-sidedness of the Truth and Reconciliation sessions, Mandela's redemptive vengeance has not totally ignored the need for justice and redeeming the past. However, the clearest example in recent history would be Martin Luther King and the Civil Rights struggle in America. As Michael Dyson has demonstrated, King's legacy has been so distorted that the real Martin has been obscured. According to Dyson, the real King, especially after 1965, was concerned with gaining reparation, with class struggle and anti-militarism.[39] For King redemption was more than just a philosophical proposition: it was a faith exemplified in a new practice.

As a theological method, redemptive vengeance makes Black rage its existential starting point and *action* its final outcome. To believe in redemptive vengeance it is necessary to recapture lost views of God within Black Churches. Later I will suggest that we need to find congruence between Black rage and faith in God, which might be expressed through a recapturing of the concept of 'rahtid'. While the theological dimensions will be discussed in the next chapter, here I wish to explore the psychological-social dimensions of redemptive vengeance.

Redemptive vengeance is concerned with making the pain of Black suffering known. As mentioned above, the last five years of the 1990s have left many Black communities and people stunned, mystified and enraged. Many people withdrew into a collective field of depression during aspects of the Lawrence case as the police ineptitude and the state complicity with racial terror unfolded on our television screens.

On the one hand, redemptive vengeance is an articulation of our outrage, anger and despair. This is necessary because a consequence of negotiating racism in Britain is that we have learned to live schizophrenic existences – we say one thing and do another, or do one thing and believe another. From slavery to the present we have learned to 'signify'[40] in this way, often as a means of survival and sometimes as a means of ridiculing 'backra'.[41] The value of signifying is not to be devalued, especially given the increased public surveillance of Black people in shopping centres, malls and places of work. But redemptive vengeance has to challenge aspects of this duplicitous process and encourage us to find progressive and liberative modes of articulating our real feelings, up front, in public as well as private. Those who have lived this kind of life know that there are risks and dangers. The example of Jesus, however, reminds us that true faith requires us to take risks for the sake of justice in the world.

On the other hand, this articulation of Black rage does not ignore internal problems within the Black community. Above, I outlined ways in which we directly or indirectly collude with the forces that fuel our rage. Because redemptive vengeance is bifocal, it does not ignore the need to give voice to the rage that is focused on what is going on within Black communities – it is also concerned with making known and making sense of the internal suffering and troubles within Black communities. Many of the victims within our communities are women and children.

Domestic violence, neglect and abuse are unhealthy areas of life that must be addressed. Unfortunately, because we live in a highly racialised society, the pain of Black women and children is given low priority and influence. However, as will be seen in Chapter 4, the hip-hop tradition of Lauryn Hill redresses this imbalance.

Finally, redemptive vengeance is an inherently positive force, which seeks to make good out of bad situations. It is not concerned with bitterness or withdrawal, but with hope and engagement. While absorbing and affirming Black rage, it does not end with it. Instead it promotes a hope located in the life of Jesus and within the witness of many of our ancestors. Because its focus is total transformation, redemptive vengeance does not seek to return evil with evil but, instead, to return evil with good. As was the case with the moral foundations of the Civil Rights Movement, redemptive vengeance realises that morally we cannot use the master's and mistress's violent tools to dismantle the master's and mistress's house. Instead, redemptive vengeance seeks to find a new pathway based on the liberating witness of Jesus. As followers of Jesus, we know that we can take the risk of faith involved in this kind of risk-taking hope, because we know that the final victory has been secured for us. In the next chapter, I will outline the theological underpinnings of redemptive vengeance.

2.
God of the rahtid: redemptive vengeance

Introduction: cussin' my White colleague

In the previous chapter I outlined the rage caused by *problematic inclusion* and *pernicious exclusion*. Building on these themes, in this chapter I want to develop a theological framework for interpreting the low-level Black rage mentioned above. I want to begin with a personal experience of rage, which is related to both of these categories. I will then attempt to analyse the rage in light of the religious-cultural analysis also outlined in the introductory chapter. I will then provide a theological framework for understanding redemptive vengeance.

In my working adult life I have only once called an individual a 'racist' to their face. I have generally avoided accusatory politics, but on this occasion after four years of the subtlest racialised hostility, I erupted. My anger was full and volcanic.

I told the person in no uncertain terms that I was leaving my present post because of his racism. He responded by saying that I had overlooked his efforts to deal with racism. I replied in no uncertain terms by suggesting that the recent despicable treatment of a Black female employee weakened, if not eradicated today's proclamation of transformation. He then switched the subject of the encounter away from my questions about structural inequality to the area of personal relationships – I have found this to be a common tactic amongst some White liberal Christians. He continued by saying that he was not fully to blame, and that our relationship going wrong was at the centre of the problem. Although there was some truth in his statement I was not willing to listen, because he had inadvertently struck a negative cord in my psycho-history.

Since childhood, I have heard Whites and some Blacks suggest that racial injustice was a Black problem. Naturally, his implying this made my blood boil. In the context of the work-place, I thought, how dare he implicate me in the multiple cases of structural racism, the derogatory language used against Black people, the numerous complaints by Black students (and some conscious White students) about the genteel hostility practised at the college? I exclaimed, 'You are a racist!' He received my wrathful words with a mixture of shock and fear. 'That is a damning indictment,' he replied. I responded with Pentecostal certitude, 'Yes it is, but it is the truth and the truth shall set you free.' With those final words, I left the room.

After reflecting on the encounter, two questions went through my mind. First, why had I taken so long to erupt? In other words, why had I suppressed my low-level rage in such a way that it resulted in this outburst? The second question was, was it possible to use this rage in a positive rather than destructive way? This second question was the result of realising that my explosion had left both my colleague and myself separated and at war.

1. Why had it taken me so long?

Regarding the first question, I am concerned with aspects of my religious-cultural experience that caused me to hold back for so long. This is an important social question that goes beyond my experiences at college. As numerous social policy documents have shown, British psychiatric hospitals and prisons are full of young African and African-Caribbean men whose psychotic episodes have their origin in complex processes and structures related to living in a racist society. I want to suggest four possible explanations for my neurosis.

Institutionalised oppression

I begin with the suffocating context of the White theological academy. White Christianity in England is proficient in suppressing Black people's rage. Its methods, developed over centuries of colonial and imperial rule over people of colour, are overwhelming. In my experience, there was evidence of cultural racism within the English Christian institution in which I worked which ensured the subordination of Black people by fixing Black cultures as 'less than' and inferior.[1] One outcome of marginalising Black cultures is to make Black people invisible. While it is possible to address this kind of new racism outside of the Church by appealing to cultural theory or even aspects of current legislation, it is nearly impossible to confront cultural racism within English Christianity. There are at least three reasons for this being the case.

First, as James Cone demonstrated in *Black Theology and Black Power*, much of White Christianity has 'legalised' cultural imperialism under the rubric of traditional Eurocentric theology.[2] Second, in many cases English Christianity has conveniently manoeuvred itself outside the framework of anti-racist legislation and practice. By hiding behind a pseudo-religious integrity many White Churches have totally ignored equal opportunities policies and practices. Third, institutionalised oppression is maintained by playing a 'waiting game' when it comes to racial justice. Let me give an illustration from theological education.

On the one hand the theological academy in Britain claims moral concern with racial justice. The saturation with the language of justice, peace and reconciliation convinces many that mere words ensure just treatment. On the other hand, it soon becomes clear from working with White theologians or worshipping in many White Churches that this saturation with the language of justice is a veneer masking inactivity and expedience. In short, racial justice is mostly teleological – something to occur in the future – rather than existential – a concrete struggle in the present. This way, the status quo of White, male Christian domination is maintained. Under such conditions, Black people in minor academic positions or some Black members of White Churches are kept in place with the false promise of change in the future. Eventually, the slow pace or non-existent change leads to a seething low-level rage amongst many Black people.

Interestingly, a by-product of the academy's racism is collusion. At the college where I worked, not all Black members of staff asked critical questions about the over-representation of Black people as kitchen-workers, toilet-cleaners and bedmakers.

'Enemy love'

The second reason for my pent-up anger was related to my Black Church conditioning. I was taught to love my enemies despite the persistence of injustice or suffering. The African-American ethicist Anthony Pinn elaborates on this kind of theology of suffering in Black Churches.

Pinn suggests that Diasporan African communities faced with injustice have three responses:

- first, that while unmerited suffering is intrinsically evil it can have redemptive consequences;
- second, God and humans are co-workers in the struggle to remove moral evil;
- third, Black suffering may result from God being racist.[3]

In the Black Church context in which I was raised, the third position (God is racist) was not an option. As I demonstrated in *Dread and Pentecostal* (SPCK, 2000) the second option, divine–human participation against injustice, was a path that we rarely trod. Instead, it was the first position, seeking redemption in suffering, that was taught within the contexts of the church and my home. Therefore racialised oppression in the form of un-employment, underemployment, structural racism at school and university were all part of a divine plan to make us stronger, fitter and better Christians. As womanist reflections on divine suffering and surrogacy have shown, there is something 'troub-ling in the soul' when the oppressed view oppression as redemptive.[4] So where did the Black Church get this teaching?

From my analysis, 'enemy love' was probably grounded in a corrupt teaching to Caribbean slaves. Certain forms of African-Caribbean Christianity taught that a literal reading of Matthew 5:38–44 (loving your enemies) would enhance personal piety.[5] Under this scheme, retribution for the wicked would come from God, beyond history. In the meantime the best that we could hope for when challenged by major evils in the world was the consolation that doing good to our enemies was like heaping burning coals upon their heads (Proverbs 25:21–2). Therefore, our 'enemy love' would have some social effect in the present. Even so, our focus was ultimately spiritual – suffering made us more proficient in our understanding and carrying out of the Gospel.

However, the problem with enemy love was that it was not connected to any meaningful quest for justice. That is to say, our suffering was only redemptive on a personal level and not related to a wider civil rights campaign geared towards social change. Hence, this version of enemy love ensured that we were generally socially unresponsive to racism. One result was the damage to the Black Christian 'street cred': we were seen as inactive in the presence of evil, suggesting that our God was at best passive and at worst a White racist.

Black professional conditioning

Third, I also stayed quiet because of class conditioning. As a Black man, who had 'made it' through ingenuity and hard work, I had adopted a particular Black professional's approach to conflict. I expected to be heard and consequently treated better and taken seriously because of my education and status.

I now recognise that such an elitist, narcissistic viewpoint was the result of a false meritocratic world-view. I actually thought that good ideas and reason would eventually be rewarded without regard to 'race'. Hence, initially it was difficult to consolidate my meritocratic ideals with the real possibility of being treated dismissively, ignored or having to play waiting games on the England's post-colonial 'level playing fields'.

Talking of post-colonial playing fields, the tragic reality for many Black professionals is brilliantly articulated in Stella Orakwue's analysis of Black professional footballers in Britain. In *Pitch Invaders* Orakwue's analysis sums up the professional footballers' dilemma: despite having made it, they are still subject to the same racialised oppression visited on other Black people. Orakwue states:

> I realised that despite their current professional and
> financial success, our top Black footballers have been
> unable to shake off the stigmas, stereotyping and racist
> labelling attached to the one thing they share in common:
> the colour of their skin. The criticisms, sniping and attacks
> levelled at them are exactly the ones thrown at the Black
> communities they came from, and which many still have
> roots in. They remain outsiders who have to contend with
> attitudes no White player comes up against . . . It seems
> that money, skill, fame and even adulation from a mainly
> White fan base can't help you escape the White legacies
> of your Black skin. Getting to the top of the pile makes
> no difference – it can even make it worse.[6]

This is not a new viewpoint on Black professional life. Joe Feagin and Melvin Sikes' study of the Black middle classes concludes that Black professional people cannot expect to be treated differently from non-professional Blacks in a White supremacist patriarchal society.[7] The Black feminist Patricia Hill Collins makes a similar claim in *Fighting Words*. Through an analysis of African American women in the workplace, Collins outlines 'a new politics of containment' concerned with policing Black professional women. As a result, 'middle-class Black women are watched to ensure that they remain "unraced" and assimilated'.[8]

What I am suggesting is that my low-level rage was also related to the harsh fact that, despite education and experience, even within theological education, in reality, within the pseudo-egalitarian framework of theological education I was still just another 'nigger'.

Pathology of Black rage

Finally, I stayed quiet because I feared being pathologised as the 'angry Black male with a chip on his shoulder'. As a Black man, I was conscious of wanting to limit my aggression and assertiveness in response to injustice. A long time before, I had made a conscious decision, in response to inner-city comprehensive schooling, to suppress my rage and find other ways to negotiate racism.

As Tony Sewell has shown in his study of Black male children in the British school system, the fear of the Black male runs deep in secondary schooling. One result is that from an early age Black males are unfairly over-policed at school.[9] Such conditioning leaves Black male children having to negotiate their resistance through conformity, rebellion or innovation.[10] One result of conformity is the repression of Black feelings, including rage.

However, my situation was also made pathological by the

fact that competing on terms that ensure Black repression often creates pathological behaviour. Kobena Mercer elaborates on this Black male double jeopardy when he states:

> There is a further contradiction, another turn of the screw of oppression, which occurs when Black men subjectively internalise and incorporate aspects of the dominant definitions of masculinity in order to contest the definitions of dependency and powerlessness which racism and racial oppression enforce.[11]

Internalising the 'master's tools' often creates dysfunctional Black men who are unable to dismantle the 'master's house'. Indeed, in my situation, the 'master's tools' entrapped me. My outburst was used to pathologise me, reinforcing a 'common sense' belief that Black folks can't keep their cool under pressure. In such circumstances a dangerous stereotype is 'read' as empirically true.

2. A Positive use of vengeance?

The second question that plagued my mind was 'Are there ways in which Black people can make use of the anger generated by injustice in such a way that it becomes a dynamic, life-giving force?' In other words, is it possible to develop a *redemptive vengeance* as part of a Black Christian spirituality? A redemptive vengeance is a way of responding to injustice that redeems both the sufferer and perpetrator. In this sense vengeance is a form of retaliation geared towards the salvation of both the 'Self' and the 'Other'. In essence redemptive vengeance is the process of returning *evil* with *good*.

This second question has two focuses, first, the need for a vision of God in Christ that makes sense of Black rage, in particular a justified low-level Black rage, which is an acceptable response to seeing and experiencing injustice. Second, locating Black rage in the teachings of Jesus.

Hermeneutics and rahtid

In order to answer these questions it is necessary to engage in a hermeneutical manoeuvre where our existential questions engage in dialogue with the biblical text. Within this interpretive schema, meaning lies primarily but not exclusively beyond the text within the life experience of the reader. Therefore, to know what God is doing in the world one must begin with an examination of the 'text of life'. Put simply, as a Black theologian, I bring my experience of rage to the Bible to see what God has to say about it. In this case, what I want to call *rahtid* existence must be thrust upon the biblical text in order to make sense of this experience.

Rahtid

For those from my parents' generation, 'rahtid' is a misunderstood word. It's used as an exclamation, 'too rahtid!'[12] It is also generally understood as what you say when you can't use a curse word. (It is similar in function to the English use of 'damn!'.) However, rahtid has transcended these parameters of first-generation African-Caribbean migrants in Britain. Hence, in culturally hybrid communities such as mine in Handsworth, Birmingham the term 'rahtid' may apply to that which is surprising or overwhelming. Even so, to suggest a relationship between God and rahtid would be greeted with at least suspicion in African-Caribbean religious circles!

But it is possible to make a link, because there is another level of meaning at work within this word. Etymologically, 'rahtid' is a Jamaican derivative of the biblical word 'wrath'. Here, to talk of something as rahtid, is to suggest anger and rage. If one accepts this meaning as the primary meaning, then by returning to the original Jamaican derivative, by bringing my experience of rage, encapsulated in the original use of rahtid, to the Bible, I want to search for a God of the rahtid. A God of the rahtid is found in the understanding of God as one who *feels* and *knows* what it means to experience righteous anger. More specifically, a God of the rahtid is a God who sides with and makes sense of Black rage in response to racialised oppression in Britain. Here, God is understood through experience – as Black feminists have shown, Black epistemologies place a premium upon knowing through experience.[13]

If 'rahtid' conceptualises a type of Black rage, is it possible to locate rahtid within the teachings of Jesus? Locating a God of the rahtid within the teachings of Jesus is important for Black Christians. This is because, as demonstrated in the studies of Black British Christianity by Valentina Alexander, Iain MacRobert and Roswith Gerloff,[14] it is the interpretations of Jesus, and also eschatology, that have done most to limit Black Christian participation in contemporary political life. In short, a view of Jesus as non-political and an 'other-worldly' eschatology have been dual forces in the production of a Black Christian political apathy.

The Kingdom of God and God of the rahtid

I want to ground the concept of a God of the rahtid in Jesus' teachings of the Kingdom of God. The Kingdom symbolises the rule of God here and now and provides a space of radical transformation where boundaries, insecurities and impossibilities are overcome. In Black Churches all over the country we sing and shout about the joy of living in the Kingdom of God because it is an exciting place for the marginalised, downtrodden and abused to find 'somebodyness', uplift and status. Black rage, when placed within the Kingdom, is refocused and redirected – Kingdom theology reformulates and reconfigures the concept of a God of the rahtid so that it becomes aligned to both spiritual renewal and socio-political transformation. In order to demonstrate how the Kingdom challenges the God of the rahtid, I will explore in brief views in the Black Church and Black theological perspectives on the place of justice in the Kingdom now and in the future.

Black theology and the Kingdom of God – realised eschatology

It is well documented in New Testament scholarship that there were many angry groups often subsumed under the heading of Zealots who desired vengeance against the Roman colonisers. The critical question is, did Jesus share their vengeful desires? In the Black British Church tradition opinion is split over this matter.

On the one hand, there are traditionalists within Black Churches who argue that divine retribution in the teachings of Jesus were for the end of the age. In the meantime, divine rule meant rule over the *hearts* of men and women.[15] Therefore, a distinction was to be made between the present (spiritual) and the future (political). However, this myopic gaze does not explore the teachings of Jesus concerned with holistic trans-formation in the present. In essence, the Kingdom being 'at hand' implies that change is taking place now.

On the other hand, there is a small radical group of academic theologians in the Black Church who view Jesus' proclamation of the arrival of the Kingdom as political. For this second camp, Jesus' announcement of divine rule was a direct challenge to Roman political authority. Therefore, today humans must participate with God in socio-political change consistent with the ethics of the Kingdom. The main difficulty with this realised eschatological camp is that they neglect the apocalyptic dimensions of Jesus' teachings and consequently reduce a fluid concept to a static one.

However, it is possible to opt for a view of the Kingdom of God in Black thought where the future vision of the Kingdom has a transformative effect in the present. Two examples from the 'old' and 'new' schools of Black theology in the USA reveal how this can happen.

Old and new school views on the Kingdom of God

From the 'old school' of the 1960s and 70s, the African American theologian James Cone argues that the Kingdom ushers in a new age for Black people. Because the Kingdom is at hand, oppressed men and women are compelled to deal with evil in the world rather than fixing their attention on the *eschaton*:

> If eschatology means that one believes that God is totally uninvolved in the suffering of men because he is preparing them for another world, then Black Theology is an earthy theology! It is not concerned with the 'last Things' but with the 'White thing'. Black Theology like Black Power believes that the self-determination of Black people must be emphasised at all costs, recognising that there is only one question about reality for Blacks: What must we do about White racism?[16]

However, despite Cone's emphasis on the immanent nature of liberation, elsewhere he accepts that liberation is *also* transcendent over history:

> It is important to note that Black theology, while taking history with utmost seriousness does not limit liberation to history. When people are bound to history, they are enslaved to what the New Testament calls the law of death . . . if the oppressed, while living in history can nonetheless see beyond it, if they can visualise an eschatological future beyond the history of their humiliation, then 'the sigh of the oppressed', to use Marx's

phrase, can become a cry of revolution against the established order.[17]

Here Cone accepts the power of the 'not yet', but only as a motivating force in the liberation struggle in the now. In other words, viewing liberation as a future event can have a powerful effect on the struggle in the present. What Cone provides for us is a vision of how it is possible for an otherworldly eschatology to secure participation in liberation praxis in the present.[18] Even so, there are several difficulties with Cone's early views, in particular, his realised eschatology failed to take seriously the internal liberation within Black communities. Women, the disabled, gay and lesbian Blacks were not part of his vision of the Kingdom on earth. As a man of his time and dealing with pressing social conditions pertaining to racial advancement, Cone was not in a position to consider a multi-dimensional view of emancipation concerned with liberation for the environment and for healing between ethnic groups, or the rich and poor.

In contrast, the 'new school' of the 1980s and 90s has attempted to redefine eschatology for second- and third-generation Black and womanist theologians living in the post-civil rights, consumerist cultures of North America and the domestic neo-colonial cultures of Europe.

For example, the womanist theologian Karen Baker-Fletcher provides a wider scope in her realised eschatology. She demands a vision of a society concerned with social and environmental renewal.[19] Most significantly, Baker-Fletcher suggests that Black eschatologies draw from holistic African worldviews where past, present and future are intertwined. That is, 'past, present and future are held together within a spiritual reality that is both immanent and transcendent.'[20] Therefore God stands outside and inside of time, as an empowering Spirit seeking harmony and wholeness for humanity and creation.[21] Here, human beings participate in the growth of the Kingdom, and are able to risk all because the future is secure. This view from the new school provides a broader and more complex eschatology where justice, love and wholeness are central to the coming of the Kingdom.

The challenge of the Kingdom of God to the God of the rahtid

Returning to the concerns of this chapter, the second and third generations' eschatological vision raises questions about the nature and practice of Black rage concealed within the concept of the God of the rahtid. This requires two points of clarification that can be summarised under the headings of compatibility and challenge.

Compatibility

First, I want to affirm compatibility between the God of the rahtid and the Kingdom of God. The God of the rahtid can be located within the thrust of the Kingdom of God only because the Kingdom is concerned with a non-oppressive future breaking into the present. Where there is a quest for justice, there is space for rage. However, the type of rage validated by the Kingdom is righteous rage. Righteous rage is the rage geared towards seeking wholeness. Righteous rage demands a broader analysis and a response to injustice which seeks to do more than redress or compensate. Instead righteous rage seeks to build a new order that makes injustices less likely. This kind of rage can be distinguished from unrighteous rage, which is geared towards petty revenge, as the 'eye for an eye, tooth for a tooth' became.

Righteous Black rage is a dimension of the Kingdom of God. This means that Black people struggling with vexation and seeking restitution can find a home within the teachings of Jesus on the Kingdom. There has long been a common-sense argument that Black theological thought cannot provide answers for 'street level' debates about Black rage. Against this, we can say that Jesus, as a God of the rahtid, 'prepares a table in the presence of our enemies' so that we are able to find strength, guidance and power to overcome.

Finally, the fact that a God of the rahtid affirms Black rage nurtures a hermeneutic of suspicion towards those who encourage us to surrender our rage. As mentioned above, inner-city comprehensive education encouraged me to repress my rage rather than find a positive articulation. Today the temptation to sacrifice black rage is just as strong. This is because the 'rewards' for remaining silent are so great. bell hooks, in *Killing Rage*, articulates the complicity of silence:

> By demanding that Black people repress and annihilate our rage to assimilate, to reap the benefits of material privilege in White supremacist patriarchal culture, White folks urge us to remain complicit with their efforts to colonise, oppress and exploit. Those of us Black people who have the opportunity to further our economic status willingly surrender our rage. Many of us have no rage.[22]

Challenge

Second, also important is the challenge of the Kingdom to aspects of the God of the rahtid. In sum, Kingdom theology requires a use of Black rage that provides 'revolutionary hope' and healing for the whole community. In order to provide revolutionary hope, the God of the rahtid *cannot* advocate orientations which are nihilistic. As shown in my experience outlined earlier, all too often Black rage leads to neurotic or psychotic episodes which, while providing short-term relief, do not deal with the underlying or long-term issues that must be alleviated. On the contrary, revolutionary hope provides a pathway for new ways of being and doing. Revolutionary hope provides the 'ways and means' for social transformation. Therefore the God of the rahtid is constructive rather than destructive and provides faith rather than despair. Under these conditions there is always the potential for Black rage to become focused, organised and compelling. bell hooks affirms this point in *Killing Rage*. She states:

> Confronting my rage, witnessing the way it moved me to grow and change, I understood intimately that it had the potential not only to destroy but also to construct. Then and now I understand rage to be a necessary aspect of resistance struggle. Rage can be a catalyst inspiring courageous action.[23]

Kingdom theology also challenges the God of the rahtid to provide healing. To talk of healing in the context of Black Britain is to be concerned not only with freedom and liberation, but also with reconciliation. In other words, as well as being concerned with setting ourselves free from the tyranny of racism, sexism and classism, it is also important to move beyond freedom to love. Moving towards love means taking seriously the need for reconciliation. Later, I will show that this is a complex process that must take into consideration the ways in which Black people are often 'conned' into bypassing freedom for the sake of a *weak reconciliation*.

Weak reconciliation is resolution without justice. It pays no attention to the past and focuses on the future. Therefore, past injustices are not corrected. Also, weak reconciliation makes no demands from the victimiser; instead it is the victim who has to cover most ground by forgiving the most and receiving the least. In contrast, *strong reconciliation* views justice as an integral component of reconciliation. In addition, strong reconciliation is concerned with past, present and future. This is because it is concerned with redeeming the past in order to secure peace and justice today and tomorrow. Strong reconciliation is hard to find, especially within the British context. Take, for example, the need to make restitution for slavery. Even the most 'Black-friendly' government in the post-war period has found itself incapable of apologising for the nation's complicity with slavery. There is still no Remembrance Day for the millions of Africans killed as a result of the English slave trade. Strong reconciliation makes demands on both the victim and the victimiser. Both have to make amends for the past in order to secure peace and love in the present and beyond.

So far in this chapter, I have made an existential connection between Black rage and the rahtid and Kingdom theology. I have suggested that within the Kingdom of God, Black rage becomes a healing force that is able to save both victim and victimiser alike. In other words, Kingdom theology transforms the God of the rahtid into a *redemptive vengeance*. In the previous chapter, I outlined the socio-political dimensions of redemptive vengeance. I will now explore redemptive vengeance as a theological category. In order to offer a more detailed explanation of redemptive vengeance as the way of the God of the rahtid it is necessary to locate redemptive vengeance on a Black British vengeance continuum. In order to do this, I will explore the theme of rage in Black Britain, by focusing on aspects the work of the dub poet Linton Kwesi Johnson. After a brief résumé of his work, I want to describe two vengeance motifs found within his canon. I will end by comparing Johnson's motifs with redemptive vengeance.

3. Redemptive vengeance and Black culture

Rage within second-generation Black British subjects such as myself has been articulated on many fronts. In the world of academia one may examine the work of social scientists and cultural critics. In popular music one may choose from a broad range of popular art forms such as reggae, rap and R & B. In addition, as a recent anthology by Lemn Sissay[24] has shown, Black rage is charted in Black British poetry. Arising from this genre is the potent work of Linton Kwesi Johnson.

Linton Kwesi Johnson

Like many of the second generation of Black radicals, Linton Kwesi Johnson (LKJ), born in Jamaica in 1952 and schooled in England, has political pedigree. In 1970 he joined the Black Panther Movement where he organised poetry workshops as a means of articulating Black struggle in the early 1970s. His work was first published in the Journal *Race Today* in 1973 and his first book, *Voices of the Living Dead*, was published in 1974. His second volume, *Dread, Beat and Blood*, was published in 1975 (Bogle-L'Ouverture). After gaining a BA in sociology from Goldsmiths College, he was eventually awarded the Cecil Day Lewis Fellowship for a writer in residence in Lambeth. It was with his third volume, *Inglan is a Bitch* (Race Today Publications, 1981) that Linton's work began to receive the critical acclaim it deserved from the wider press.

I remember the first LKJ album I heard. It was *Dread, Beat and Blood*, in 1979. As a teenager wrestling with school racism, Black identity and culture, I was entranced by the potent mixture of dub music, political commentary and social analysis. Here was a poet able to articulate and analyse contemporary issues with humour and power. The lyrical power was transmitted through dub music. Johnson expresses the power of the music in the poem 'Bass Culture':

> it is di beat of di heart
> this pulsing of blood
> that is a bubblin bass
> a bad bad beat
> pushin gainst di wall
> whey bar black blood[25]

Analysis, performance and rage

Why is LKJ so important in a religious-cultural analysis of rage? First, there is the importance of his social analysis.

D'Aguiar, in the introduction to the collection of poems by LKJ provocatively entitled *Inglan is a Bitch*, rightly assesses the significance of LKJ when he suggests that:

> Not since Shelley had England seen a poet whose
> sense of craft was part and parcel of his engagement in
> the most testing political issue of the day: the SUS laws,
> unemployment, civil rights campaigns, racism, youth
> culture and the growth of a Black middle class to name a
> few.[26]

The brilliance of LKJ is found in his ability to explore complex social issues through dub poetry. Whether it was an unjust imprisonment, racist attack or immigration policy, LKJ is able to present a Black perspective on the issue to challenge, strengthen and educate the listener. Such a gift is scarce.

Second, LKJ is significant because he mobilises both performance and the languages of the Black community. Regarding performance, dub poetry is a powerful medium for communicating ideas. As Beth-Sarah Wright has demonstrated, performance poetry such as 'dub' poetry is part of complex interplay between identity, culture and politics. She states:

> As a genre heavily imbued with both orality and
> performance techniques, it embodies a sensory modality
> capable of evoking strong collective responses,
> challenging assumptions of historical authenticity,
> disseminating knowledge and heightening cultural
> awareness.[27]

Regarding language, by utilising both Black British and Jamaican language, Johnson reinstates meaning in language considered alien, improper and substandard. Johnson paved the way for the acceptance of black 'twang' – Black British language that goes beyond the boundaries of the Black community. Because in Johnson's canon Black language is the vehicle for articulating the struggles of Black people, he functions as one of Antonio Gramsci's 'organic intellectuals',[28] articulating the revolutionary aspirations of the Black community:

> The language shows the members of Britain's Black working class to be radicalised by their own experiences and the political sense they made of them. From this standpoint, the poet aligns himself with them and becomes a messenger as much as a visionary on their behalf.[29]

Third, in my opinion, LKJ is important because of his rage. In a social context where virtuous and committed Black leaders have been hard to find or have disappeared as quickly as they arrived, Johnson has stood fast as a critical voice and a chief spokesperson on Black rage. With unfaltering consistency he has expressed the common outrage, disgust and discontent of Black men and women in Britain. When no one dared to speak out in public or found that there were no words to express our feelings, Johnson appeared with a poem capturing our mood. Nowhere is Johnson's ability sharper than in his analysis of policing.

He has given voice to numerous accounts of police injustice, from the ill treatment of George Lindo in the poem 'It Dread in a Inglan' to the alleged framing of Darcus Howe articulated in the poem 'Man Free'. Furthermore, his critique of the SUS law in the anti-SUS poem 'Sonny's Lettah' captured the rage and anguish felt by the majority of second-generation Black Britons in the early 1980s. More recently, 'Liesense fi Kill' on his album *More Time* captures the contemporary mood concerning the murder of Black people in police custody in Britain. However, analysing Johnson from a Black Christian political perspective raises several problems with Johnson's art form and its contents.

Critique

Regarding style, while Johnson is a first-rate analyst, his work lacks the philanthropic 'black love' necessary for challenging and humanising Black people. I am not saying that Linton does not love his people, but what I am suggesting is that this kind of love is not always expressed in his writings. In order to understand this point it is necessary to turn to the patriarch of Black rage, Malcolm X. Malcolm X showed that Black analysis needed to be wedded to love of one's people. The African-American cultural critic Cornel West, commenting on Malcolm's love of his people, states:

> Malcolm X was a prophet of Black rage primarily because of his great love for black people. His love was neither abstract nor ephemeral. Rather, it was a concrete connection with a degraded and devalued people in need of psychic conversion. This is why Malcolm X's articulation of black rage was not directed first and foremost against white America. Rather, Malcolm believed that if black people felt the love that motivated that rage, the love would produce a psychic conversion in black people, they would find themselves as human beings, no longer viewing their bodies, minds and souls through white lenses, and believing themselves capable of taking control of their own destinies.[30]

In contrast, Johnson's rage, in my analysis, is driven by injustice in racist Britain and a desire to mobilise black people. Without an explicit expression of Malcolm's pan-African *agape*, LKJ's work lacks the humanising force necessary to succeed in the mobilising task. While his work is important, it does not always motivate or inspire action from the masses.

Regarding content, another critical concern is LKJ's critique of religion. Like many Black British sociologists and cultural critics Johnson fails to see the importance of religious reflection as a tool in social analysis. Instead, like many of his intellectual generation, he views religion as an opiate. For example, in 'Reality Poem', Johnson suggests that religion provides an escape for those unwilling to deal with the critical political situation:

> W'en wi can't face reality
> Wi leggo wi clarity
> Some latch an to vanity
> Some hol' insanity
> Some get vision
> Start preach relijan
> But dem can't mek dicishan
> W'en it come to wi fite
> Dem can't mek dicishan
> W'en it comes to wi rites

What I am suggesting is that, like many political nationalists, LKJ fails to acknowledge the role of Black Christianity in nineteenth- and twentieth-century African continental and diasporan resistance. By omitting spirituality from his discourse he fails to explore fully the various ways in which Black people negotiate racialised oppression.

Spirituality is a major force in contemporary Black British life. One only has to review recent records on church attendance to see that Black Christianity is alive and thriving in Britain. Likewise, the growth of Islam, both orthodox and the Nation of Islam, in urban areas also bears witness to the growing power of religion amongst second- and third-generation Black youth. In addition, the increased production of written texts and conferences on Black women's spirituality in Black Atlantic cultures shows that even outside of traditional religion, Black faith is being explored and applied to Black life. One cannot do comprehensive cultural or political work on Black existence and ignore the importance of Black religion and spirituality.

LKJ and vengeance

Finally, despite the limitations expressed from a Black Christian political perspective, there is much to be gained from an analysis of Johnson's work. Of great importance to this study is Johnson's approach to vengeance. I want to show that he provides two vengeance motifs. In order to explain these motifs I have drawn from the work of the Black South African theologian Willa Boesak. Through a study of the post-apartheid period, Boesak explores the validity of *punitive* and *corrective* justice as tools for alleviating the suffering of the masses.[31] I want to suggest that Johnson's canon contain similar themes in terms of vengeance.

Punitive vengeance

First, punitive vengeance. Punitive vengeance is concerned with retribution. The central theme is that retaliation is a legitimate response to crimes committed against the community and the individual. In the case of LKJ, there is a strand in his canon which suggests that he is concerned with responding to force with force, violence with violence. This belief is predicated upon the assumption that fascist or racist behaviour is the result of a lack of intelligence. Therefore, there is no reason to use one's intellect in response to racist behaviour:

> We gonna smash their brains in
> Cause they ain't got nofink in 'em
> We gonna smash their brains in
> Cause they ain't got nofink in 'em

However, for Johnson, punitive vengeance is fundamentally defensive action. The moral justification for such action is the right to defend ourselves against the unprovoked attacks made upon the Black community. The only legitimate response is to fight and drive back fascist attack:

some a dem say dem a niggah haytah
an' some a dem say dem a black betah
some a dem say dem a black stabah
an' some a dem say dem a paki bashah
fashist an di attack
no baddah worry 'bout dat
fashist an di attack
wi wi' fite dem back
fashist an di attack
den wi countah-attack
fashist an di attack
den wi drive dem back

In addition to fascist attack, defensive action is also a legitimate response to police brutality. In 'All Wi Doin is Defendin',
from the *Forces of Vicktry* album, punitive vengeance is the
consequence of the inability of the police to heed prior warnings:

War . . . war . . .
Mi say lissen
Oppressin man
Hear what I say if yu can
Wi have
A grevious blow fi blow

Wi will fite you in di streets wid wi han
Wi have a plan
Soh lissen man
Get ready fi tek some blows
Doze days
Of di truncheon
An doze nites of melancholy locked in a cell
Doze hours of torture tuchin hell
Doze blows dat cause my heart to swell
Were well

Numbered
And are now at an end

All wi doin
Is defendin
So get yu ready
Fi war . . . war . . .
Freedom is a very firm thing . . .

Here punitive vengeance has a goal: it is time for the oppressor to feel the pain of the oppressed so that their vengeance is satisfied.

The central problem with punitive vengeance is that it fails to break the cycle of violence. If violence begets violence, then there is little room for transformation that goes beyond the surface. Furthermore, as Miroslav Volf has shown,[32] if freedom is the ultimate goal in the liberation struggle, then the chances for holistic transformation are limited. This is because freedom does not deal constructively with those who are defeated; it may simply produce new oppressors. We will explore this idea further when exploring praxis for redemptive vengeance. I turn to the second use of vengeance in Johnson's work, that is, corrective vengeance.

Corrective vengeance

Corrective vengeance is the use of force to correct an injustice. Whereas punitive vengeance avenges the wickedness of the oppressor by returning in equal measure the pain inflicted upon the oppressed, corrective vengeance is concerned with gaining compensation. Corrective vengeance has a long history in Black liberal societies of the Black Atlantic. For example, Civil Rights movements, anti-colonial struggles and reparations movements are all founded upon a principle of correction of unjust laws and practices. Once injustice is acknowledged, it is necessary to compensate to appease the victim and simultaneously allow the perpetrator to pay for their acts.

Corrective vengeance is strongest in the poem 'Liesense fi kill' on the *More Time* album. Here, in a conversation between two characters, there is a discussion on the alleged ability of the police to kill Black people with impunity:

> Sometiem mi tink mi coe-workah crazy
> di way Kristeen woodah gwaan jokey-jokey
> den a nex time now a no-nonsense stance
> di way she wine-dung di place lass krismus dance
> di way she love fi taak bout conspirahcy
>
> mi an Kristeen inna di canteen a taak
> bout di det a black people inna custidy
> ow nat a cat mek meow ar a dyam daag baak
> ow nohbady high-up inna society
> can awfah explaneashan nar remidy
>
> wen Kristeen nit-up her brow
> like seh a rhow shi agoh rhow
> screw-up her face
> like seh a trace shi agoh trace
> hear her now:
>
> yu tink a jus hem-high-five an James Ban
> an poleece an solja ovah nawt highalan wan
> wen it come to black people Winston
> some poleece inna inglan got liesense fi kill

The high point of the poem is a catalogue of atrocities against Black people in police custody as proof of the licence to kill:

> an shi seh yu waan proof

yu cyaan awsk Clinton McCurbin
bout im haxfixiashan
an yu cyaan awsk Joy Gardner
bout her sufficaeshan
yu cyaan awsk Colin Roach
if im really shoot imself
an yu cyaan awsk Vincent Graham
if a im stab imself
but yu can awsk di Commishinah
bout di liesense fi kill
awsk Sir Paul Condon
bout di liesense fi kill
yu cyaan awsk di Douglas dem
bout di new style batan
an you cyaan awsk Tunay Hassan
bout im det by niglect
yu cyaan awsk Marlon Downes
if im hav any regret
an yu cyaan awsk El Gammal
bout di mistri a im det
but yu can awsk Dame Barbara
bout di liesense fi kill
awsk di DPP
bout di liesense fi kill

yu cyaan awsk Ibrahima
bout di CS gas attack
an yu cyaan awsk Missis Jarrett
ow shi get her hawt-attack
yu cyaan awsk Oliver Price
bout di grip roun im nek
an yu cyaan awsk Steve Boyce
bout im det by niglect
but yu can awsk di PCA
bout di liesense fi kill

awsk di ACPO
bout di liesense fi kill

yu fi awsk Maggi Tatcha
bout di liesense fi kill
yu can awsk Jan Mayja
bout di liesense fi kill
yu fi awsk Mykel Cowad
bout di liesense fi kill
an yu can awsk Jak Straw
bout di rule af law
yu fi awsk Tony Blare
if im is aware ar if im care
bout di liesense fi kill
dat plenty poleece feel dem gat

The benefit of corrective vengeance is change. By changing law or behaviour it is hoped that the 'system' will be corrected and future injustice prevented. The central problem with LKJ's corrective vengeance, however, is that although the victim is appeased through compensation or legislation, there is little room for the holistic transformation of the oppressor apart from financial and legal penalties. One theme that emerges from my analysis of conflict in theological education is that division and pain must be healed. In this respect, corrective vengeance fails to enact the heart change required for the holistic vision found within the concept of the God of the rahtid.

Despite the limitations found within his canon, Johnson raises important questions for Black theologians, namely, what kind of vengeance motif is utilised in our eschatological thought. In other words, how does the Kingdom here and now capture Black rage so that it becomes a positive force? This brings me to my final point, redemptive vengeance.

4. Redemptive vengeance

So is there a way in which Black people faced with nail bombs, stabbings, beatings, and institutionalised racism can react so as to produce fruit consistent with the life of the Spirit? I want to suggest that the only credible view of vengeance, not found in LKJ, is redemptive vengeance. Redemptive vengeance is 'the way of the God of the rahtid'. Whereas the Bible tells us that the ultimate act of vengeance belongs to God (Romans 12:19–21), I want to advocate that Black people must develop a form of redemptive vengeance for the here and now. Redemptive vengeance is a positive response to racialised oppression.

Saving ourselves

The first task of redemptive vengeance must be to save us. First and foremost we have an obligation to ensure that we as Black people are rescued from the multiple forms of oppression that confront us. What I want to focus on here is spiritual rescue, namely how we, as spiritual beings, save ourselves. In response to this question, I suggest that redemptive vengeance as the way of the God of the rahtid means that vengeance must have at its heart a call to repentance. Repentance is concerned with making a *return to our source*, which is, returning to God. This is the ultimate act of rescue because, as commonly acknowledged in Black popular culture, 'only God can save us'! So why should we engage with this process of return?

Firstly, because those of us fighting against racism must ensure that we are not enveloped by hate or envy. We must make sure that our hearts are turned towards God and not consumed by an unrighteous anger, which will result in self-destruction. Secondly, the teachings of Jesus are not partial in terms of who needs to repent. Those who have been victims are also asked to consider Matthew 6:24: 'Love your enemies and pray for those who persecute you.' This is particularly pertinent to my experience recounted at the beginning of the chapter where the encounter at the college left me bitter, angry and enraged. Bitterness, anger and rage, while in that context important to express, are not fruits of the Spirit! In my case, on one level, repentance meant dealing with these negative feelings in order to save myself through an act of returning to my source, that is, God.

Saving ourselves has numerous benefits. Being free of feelings of malice and anger has psychological and social benefits, for example benefits to health. In addition, saving ourselves through returning to our source means that we can make space for creative transformation. Repentance makes space for the transformation of the victim's circumstances; it provides the creative space for the repentance of the victimiser. Only through the creation of a new space as a result of repentance will the cycle of revenge, bitterness and violence cease.

Creating an environment for change

Thirdly, because redemptive vengeance is concerned with saving Black people from the negative effects of Black rage, creating an environment for change is also important. An essential ingredient here is forgiveness. Now, I am well aware of the fact that corrupt views on forgiveness are often used as part of a theological system that forces Black people to forgive injustices without demanding change by the perpetrators. In other words, within our history and experience there have been obligations laid on us which suggest that justice and forgiveness are mutually exclusive.

However, forgiveness with a call for justice is a necessary part of the process of creating an environment for change. In order to make sure that we are not consumed with hate or envy we must also 'forgive those who have sinned against us' (Matthew 6:11). On the one hand, forgiveness, that is, not bearing ill will or ill feeling towards those who have committed and continue to commit atrocities against us, does not mean that we neglect demands for reparations. On the other hand, it does mean that we go beyond the compensatory vengeance by recognising that we must check our hearts and motives as part of our quest for compensation. Compensation is not negotiable. When the 'shalom' of the community has been broken, restitution is required. Paul is aware of this theological principle in his letter to Philemon.

Writing to Philemon, Paul argues that Philemon should reinstate Onesimus. What is intriguing for me is the fact that Paul offers to 'repay' to Philemon compensation for the losses he has suffered through Onesimus' absence (v.19). Paul realised that when people are treated unjustly, integral to forgiveness is the act of reparation. Unfortunately, in relation to their crimes against humanity perpetrated in slavery and colonialism, this view has not been embraced by English Christian religion or the British State. As a result there are moral questions that arise which in effect limit the possibility of holistic reconciliation. For example, commenting on the role of reparations in the story of Onesimus, the African-American New Testament scholar Allen Dwight Callahan states:

> When a dept of injustice is incurred, justice calls for the retirement of that debt. The check must be paid. But if that debt is not retired, or as Martin Luther King put in his speech in front of the Lincoln Memorial in 1963, that check is returned stamped 'insufficient funds', the debtor remains morally bankrupt. Indeed, as long as the debt remains outstanding, there can be no more business as usual.[33]

Black people concerned with creating an environment for change can be assured that forgiveness will ensure our wellbeing but also provide space for the transformation of the victimiser.

For example, the story of Zacchaeus (Luke 19:1–10) shows us that forgiveness makes space for justice. Zacchaeus, when forgiven by Jesus, offers half of his goods to the poor and repays fourfold those he has cheated. While the fundamental aim of forgiveness is the moral and spiritual rejuvenation of Black people wronged by racialised oppression, forgiveness can also result in a returning and repaying of more than what was taken unjustly by the victimiser. What I hope to establish here is that forgiveness is *not* a substitute for justice but, instead, leads to authentic justice. However, the recent results of the Truth and Reconciliation inquiry in South Africa reveal the difficulties of repentance on the part of some oppressors. In other words, we can't 'hold our breath' in hope that restitution will come once forgiveness occurs and the environment is created for new beginnings.

New beginnings

Fourthly, to secure the effects of creating a new space for new relations to begin, room must be provided for reconciliation. Indeed, one purpose of repentance and forgiveness is reconciliation. Reconciliation marks new beginnings because without it both victim and victimiser are scarred by the act of oppression. Liberation theologians have attempted with varying degrees of success to articulate the need and role of reconciliation in the liberation quest. More often than not, liberation theology has focused on freedom rather than love as the final goal. Freedom, while breaking the chains, does not always heal the rifts that cause future generations to hate. Gustavo Gutiérrez provides some insight into this problem when he suggests that it is love, not freedom, that is the ultimate goal of the liberation struggle. Gutiérrez realises that without love humans are estranged from both God and each other.[34] The African-American feminist bell hooks sides with Gutiérrez in her book on love. hooks argues that the power and will to love has been lost in contemporary

societies. As a consequence the art and importance of reconciliation has significantly diminished in contemporary Civil Rights
and Black Nationalist circles.[35]

Once again, it is important to restate that making love a
focus in redemptive vengeance does not mean that we abandon
the quest for concrete justice; instead, we bring our trajectory
back into focus. The older Malcolm X realised this more than
any other leader in African diasporan history – that love and
justice were companions on the road to a healthy society. In
relation to the concept of a God of the rahtid, love identifies the
need for a universal and holistic reconciliation. Reconciliation
becomes possible when we return to our source and make space
for new beginnings. All of which shows that redemptive
vengeance is an active force for the Black people in Britain.

Active force

Finally, I want to affirm the fact that redemptive vengeance
is both dynamic and active. It is dynamic in the sense that it is
a process without boundaries or fixed points. That is to say,
redemptive vengeance can be reconfigured and reworked to
meet the needs of each new generation. Hence, while I am
leaving a blueprint for Black resistance, the outline is not set in
stone. Redemptive vengeance is also active. It is not concerned
with leaving the quest for justice or liberation in the hands of
the British establishment or the White Church. Instead, the
responsibility lies with us. The action that we take can be
expressed in a variety of forms. Some may choose to work from
within, others may choose to work from outside of the Church
or government. Whatever pathway is chosen, the action motif
in redemptive vengeance encourages us to 'do the right thing'.

As shown in *Jesus is Dread*, I side with the independent-
action tradition of Black struggle, that led to the development
of Black Churches in the post-war years. Such a tradition makes
its starting point Black experience. As Molefi Kete Asante

argues, it is necessary for us to search inside of ourselves to find solutions to the problems that beset us. Here I am supporting a prioritising of critical tools which emerge from our subjective experience, its ways of knowing (epistemology) and practices. This approach also advocates mobilising the people.

As Foucault has demonstrated, power relationships are changed from the bottom up rather than the top down. This means that the quest for redemption fuelled by Black rage is in the hands of everyday Black people. The challenge to Black theologians and religionists is to enable Black men and women to rework and live out redemptive vengeance in the social spaces where the rage engendered by problematic inclusion and pernicious inclusion is experienced. The task of the 'Black Theology and Black Incarceration' project established in 1999 at Birmingham prison is one such example.

As will be demonstrated in greater depth in Chapter 5, the project utilises Black film as a catalyst for theological discussion and the formulation of good practice. The central aim of the project is to provide a context for Black men to explore politics, culture and religion as tools for reform and redirection. For many of the men it was the first opportunity to explore ways in which they could control and challenge the norms that lead to exclusion and sometimes brutality. Redemptive vengeance challenges theologians, Church leaders and Church workers to be actively involved in transforming the schools, workplaces and communities and prisons where we live. The responsibility is with us.

Conclusion

In this chapter, I have attempted to provide a theological framework for redemptive vengeance. I have suggested that Black rage resonates with the African-Caribbean concept of rahtid. Therefore it is necessary to find a God of the rahtid. A space for God of the rahtid was located within the teachings of Jesus, in particular his teachings about the Kingdom of God. The Kingdom provides a space where rahtid was both affirmed and challenged. On one level the Kingdom acknowledges the cries of the victimised and downtrodden. Because the Kingdom is at hand, there is a place of rest and renewal. On another level, the Kingdom demands that rahtid make its focus redemptive vengeance. Distinguished from punitive and corrective vengeance in Black popular cultures, redemptive vengeance is concerned with wholeness, that is returning to the source of life, creating space for transformation and new beginnings. As an active force engaged with the daily struggle for Black humanity, redemptive vengeance is a radical alternative concerned with personal and communal advancement. In the next three chapters, I want to provide living examples of redemptive vengeance at work. I will begin by exploring redemptive vengeance on a personal level, that is, dealing with the history of oppression incarcerated within my slave surname, 'Beckford'.

3.
Name droppin': redeeming a slave name

Introduction

In this chapter, I want to explore redemptive vengeance on a personal level. This is because I want to show that redemptive vengeance is not some obscure religious-cultural ideal but, instead, a concrete process in which everyday people can become involved. Likewise, I want to show that redemptive vengeance is tied up with who we are and how we understand ourselves as part of the Africa diaspora.

If the personal is political, is this also true of the names we have? My name is Robert Beckford. This may not sound very significant at a first hearing. But for those 'in the know' my surname is common in both the Jamaican and British telephone directories. Which means I could be Jamaican, British, or both. Well, as part of the African-Caribbean diaspora in Britain, I occupy the 'or both' category. This is not an easy space to occupy. Upon further analysis my surname, as with many other Black people, is an historical and ideological battleground. Let me explain.

Names are important in African diasporan communities. They tell our history and, as a dimension of culture, represent a cultural journey from Africa to post-colonial England. This kind of cultural journeying is expressed in Stuart Hall's analysis of cultural identities: 'Cultural identities come from somewhere, have histories . . . identities are the names we give to the different ways we are positioned by, and position ourselves within, the narratives of the past.'[1]

In Black British communities the relationship between positioning and identity is central to the process of naming. For example, many of my parents' generation were named after famous English people. Hence names such as Winston, Leonard, Mary or Elizabeth all featured in some way in the naming process.[2] Many of my parents' generation were also named after biblical characters such as Naomi, Samson or Joseph due to the influence of English Christianity on Caribbean societies. However, a radical shift has taken place amongst second- and third-generation Black British, who choose to name their children in more creative ways.

Some went back to Africa to find forenames from African places, tribes and names in order to reconnect their offspring to their African past. For example, I have friends who named their child 'Ashanti', and another family with a child called 'Kush'. Some of my friends changed their English forenames for African ones. I know of people who were named by their Jamaican parents with ordinary names like Jennifer, Mary and Sam, but opted to change these names to the likes of Assata, Kembe and Kwame.

Other second-generation Black British 'created' names from the African diasporan oral tradition. One only needs to look at the register from any school in the Black community to see a plethora of creative and beautiful-sounding names designating second- and third-generation African-Caribbean children. 'Kai', 'Ashay' and 'Tinay' are among the names of children in one of the Sunday school classes at my church. However, despite our willingness to find new 'Christian names', we have generally been unwilling to investigate the legacy of our surnames, namely the 'brand' that we carry as a reminder of our slave past. This process is of great importance because how we describe ourselves, and our 'names', have power in defining who we are and how we understand ourselves.

For me, the issue of my surname became apparent after watching the first episode of Alex Haley's *Roots* in the late 70s. Even at 13, I had never before thought much about the significance of Black surnames. I had wrongly assumed that African-Caribbean names, like those of other ethnic groups, were the product of a natural course of history far removed from slavery and ownership. But *Roots* put an end to this myth in my young mind. Watching for the first time on television slaves being brought from Africa to the New World, and having their names changed as part of a process of subjugation, was a life-transforming event. I will never forget Kunta Kinti being beaten until he called himself by his new slave name. The programme made me realise two things about my surname 'Beckford'. First, that it signified a brutal history of subjugation, in particular, the dehumanisation of African people. Second, the name tied me not only to a problematic past but also to a White English family of which I knew nothing. In other words, a part of my heritage was to be found somewhere in England.

As a teenager living in contemporary Britain with little if any analysis of colonialism it was easy to be unaware of the profound significance of my name. However, once I began to question its status and utility, I began to feel a sense of alienation and estrangement from my surname. I began to experience a sense of diasporan longing for reconnection to an African identity and surname, which had been stolen from my ancestors. For the first time, I began to imagine myself in exile. bell hooks summarises this sense of being away from home in *Art on My Mind*, when she states:

> Everyone forgets that when we talk about Black people living in the diaspora, we're talking about a people who live in exile, and that in some ways, like all other exiles, we imagine home, we imagine journeys of return. We embark on such journeys by first looking for traces – by engaging

the palimpsest that reveals the multilayered nature of our experience.[3]

As I mentioned at the beginning of this chapter, my surname is the site of a historical and ideological battleground. However, at 34, in light of redemptive vengeance and with time, experience and funding, I decided to embark on a journey to explore the meaning that lies behind my surname. As I began this journey, I was not sure if it would be a case of 'wandering', or 'return'. Wandering would mean lots of thought and not much progress on this matter – thinking it through but ending up feeling indifferent. The only benefit would be that my identity would have been challenged, explored and possibly 'reworked' by the experience. What worried me was the realisation that tracing and retelling our stories does not always bring us closer to the past because, as Anthony Pinn has so rightly deciphered: 'With each articulation of these cultural memories, they are moved that much further from the moment of their conception and their cultural context.'[4] In contrast, I hoped that this journey would bring me closer to a place called *home*. In this sense 'return' would mean finding a sense of belonging. But I was also haunted by the 'myth of return' – the possibility of never finding home and having to live culturally, spiritually and physically in exile.

Before beginning this process, a few words of caution are necessary. First, historical distance and historical perspective make recovering the history of my name difficult. There are no clear-cut historical records connecting me with a direct and transparent genealogy. Historical distance makes the construction of the past a very difficult and fragile process. Hence, all I can hope to do is to seek insight into an already loose historical and cultural history. Second, I approach this redemptive task from a particular Black theological and political perspective and social location. I have a bias towards redeeming the past in order to make sense of the present. Even so, the longing that I have to redeem this situation is something that neither distance nor social location could wipe out.

1. Slave names and redemptive vengeance

So how do I, as a conscious Black man living in the early part of the twenty-first century, make sense of my slave name? Redemption must involve forgiveness and restitution, and be governed by the understanding of love outlined in the previous chapter. In addition, because redemption is active it must be manifested in a new praxis. As shown above, in Black Atlantic cultures a name change can signify the desire for a new praxis. Name change as redemption is also apparent within the biblical tradition. As part of the process of growth and renewal God renames people. For example, in the Old Testament Jacob becomes Israel (Genesis 32:28) and in the New Testament Simon becomes Peter (Luke 6:14). In both cases the name change has deep social, political and theological significance. The use of biblical names amongst African converts to Christianity today is testimony to the continuation of this biblical tradition. And yet, Africans taking on Christian European names as a sign of redemption does not work as well from my vantage point. For me, such a process does not effectively deal with the stain of slavery and the quest for a redeeming of this history. As a consequence many diasporan Africans are travelling in a different direction to their Christian counterparts in the continent of Africa.

In the journey of redemption, Africa offers another option: Africa as the land of redemption was popularised in nineteenth-century movements such as Ethiopianism, which is still a feature of African diasporan communities in the Northern Hemisphere. Even in the recent 'Hype' Williams film, *Belly*, Africa takes on a magical, mythical quality for a group of affluent Black urban gangsters. One of the characters, 'Sincere' (Nas), after reading *Message to the Black Man* by Elijah Mohammed, dreams of taking his wife Tionne (Tionne Watkins / T-Bos) and baby to the land of his forefathers, Africa. Africa becomes a place of freedom and redemption compared with the brutality of urban America. In my case, African redemption would mean going back to my roots.

Another option involves going beyond Africa – in other words, seeking out a new name and new praxis which emerges from the *route* that has shaped many African-Caribbean people's identities, in particular, the history and politics that lie behind our slave names. After all, if redemptive vengeance is to make any sense, it must try to redeem slavery. Such a task is complex and cannot be tackled in its entirety here. What I want to do is focus on redeeming my slave name by tracing the journey from slavery to the present.

Redeeming slavery is not an easy task. Caribbean societies, former colonial powers, theologians and Black Churches fail to take on board this history. Caribbean societies rarely venture into the antagonistic politics of reparations so central to this history. I am surprised that reparations are not a major concern in academic circles in the Caribbean. It is as though independence from former slave-holding nations in the 1960s was enough. Moreover, the favoured trading status that enabled many Caribbean countries to sell their 'cash crops' at a good rate and likewise send students to European nations seems to have appeased any major movement for a more comprehensive restitution. A similar willingness to 'let sleeping dogs lie' occurs in the former colonial countries also. No government in post-war British history has dared to deal with this tragic and barbaric episode. Moreover, theologians have also failed to address this genocide and as a consequence fail to get to grips with racism. As James Cone mentions:

> Whereas this silence has been partly broken in several

secular disciplines, theology remains virtually mute. From Jonathan Edwards to Walter Rauschenbusch and Reinhold Niebuhr to the present, progressive White theologians, with few exceptions, write and teach as if they do not need to address the radical contradiction that racism creates for Christian theology. They do not write about slavery, colonialism, segregation, and the profound cultural link these crimes created between White supremacy and Christianity.[5]

However, the critique of White theologians might also be levied against Black Churches in Britain where there is an unwillingness to address how the slave past impacts upon present domestic policy. Shockingly, amongst my parents' generation many refused to tell their children what they knew about their colonial past and slave heritage through fear. I remember a Black Church minister who once said during his sermon that he refused to tell his children about slavery and colonialism because it would make them hate White people. While one may disagree with his remedy (silence) there is some truth within his analysis, namely, the power of the historical memory to enrage in the present.

Redemption and historiography

However, a redemptive vengeance demands a liberative historiography. A liberative historiography comprises two central features: willingness to retell and willingness to seek hope and reconciliation as a result. The willingness to retell is important because, without an exploration of the meaning of our slave past, it becomes impossible to counter the negative ripples still being felt by African and African diasporan peoples. In sum, there can be no justice today without dealing with the memory. Retelling is a strategic device in the outmanoeuvring of oppression:

There can be no justice without memory – without

remembering the horrible crimes committed against humanity and the great human struggles for justice. But oppressors always try to erase the history of their crimes and often portray themselves as the innocent ones. Through their control of the media and religious, political, and academic discourse 'they're able' as Malcolm [X] put it, 'to make the victim look like the criminal and the criminal to look like the victim'.[6]

The willingness to seek hope and reconciliation emerges out of the willingness to retell. This kind of historiography seeks ways of changing life for the better as a result of retelling. This is why retelling must bear fruit – the fruit of forgiveness and repentance. For Black people the central concern must be with the restitution that accompanies repentance. This is because we have in the past been too willing to forgive without pursuing the repentance of those who have victimised us. This focus is what puts the 'liberative' into historiography!

The journey to redeem my slave name has three stages. It begins with a symbolic analysis of the trans-Atlantic journeys of my parents and ancestors. Next come the stories of my Black and White ancestors and relatives in Jamaica and England. The final part is an evaluation of the name 'Beckford' – does it stay or go as a consequence of this history?

2. The Atlantic metaphysic

The journey to redeem – to make sense of my name and interrogate its salvific relevance for me today – begins with going to Jamaica to search for the Black and White origins of my surname. To get to Jamaica requires a literal and symbolic journey across the Atlantic.

In the seventeenth, eighteenth and nineteenth century, the Atlantic was a middle passage for African slaves, sold into slavery by some of their peers and packed into slave ships to make a perilous journey to the slave plantations in the so-called 'New World'.

The Atlantic is an important ideological space for African-Caribbean people. As Vincent Harding suggests in *There is a River*, the Atlantic crossing represents a space of turmoil and terror, but also innovation, rebellion and survival. Stories of terror and its overcoming are exemplified in the story of the slave ship *Zong* in the late eighteenth century:

> The *Zong*, owned by the Liverpool banker and slave-trader William Gregson and his partners, sailed from Sao Tome, an island off the coast of what is now Gabon, on 6 September 1781. The ship was bound for Jamaica with a crew of 17 and a cargo of about 470 slaves. By 29 November seven of the crew and over 60 of the slaves were dead, and many of the other slaves were sick and unlikely to live much longer. The master of the vessel, Luke Collingwood, told his officers that if the sick slaves died a natural death the ship's owners would have to bear the loss . . . If however, the slaves were thrown alive into the sea, on the pretext that the ship's safety demanded it, the underwriters must stand the loss. Such, indeed, was the law. The mate, James Kelsal, opposed Collingwood's plan, but was told that 'it would not be so cruel to throw the poor sick wretches into the sea, as to suffer them to linger out a few days under the disorders with which they were afflicted'. The captain personally picked out 133 slaves and ordered the crew to throw them over-board. This was done in batches. Fifty-four were thrown into the sea that day and 43 the next: one of the second batch members managed to grasp a rope, climbed back into the ship undetected and survived. On the third day the remaining 36 put up a fight, so they were shackled before being drowned. The last ten victims succeeded in pulling

away from their captors and chose to die as heroes. They jumped over the side.[7]

Who really knows how many millions of Black bodies lie buried beneath the sea and how many stories of resistance and overcoming have never been recorded?

In more recent years the journey across the Atlantic is fecund with meaning for the African-Caribbean diaspora. The Atlantic represents a space crossed by Black people in search of betterment. This is a familiar space in my family history. A generation ago Black people from the so-called 'West Indies' travelled to Britain as migrant workers with the unrealistic aim of staying for a few years and making enough money to return home and live well. Unfortunately, there was only room at the bottom of England's employment ladder, and many had to settle for underemployment in some of the least desirable industries.

My parents' crossing

My father came to England first. He came by air. Being a storyteller, on many winter nights during power cuts in the 1970s he would repeat the story of his crossing. When we were children we were told fantastic stories about a plane journey from Jamaica to England in 1963. He told us of a dangerous flight in which the aeroplane landed with only one engine working! My father helped with the survival plans alongside the plane officials and ensured the safety of passengers. I've never been able to prove how factual his story is. But the part that stuck with me most was his description of his first sight of London from the air. As a rural proletarian Jamaican in his early twenties, England represented hope and opportunity: 'When I saw the buildings dem, I thought, "there must be a lot of work here".' Like his African ancestors my father crossed the Atlantic as an economic unit. He was a part of Jamaica's surplus labour created by the economic exploitation of the country by Britain. Unlike his

African ancestors, he had to pay a fare and also had some, if rather limited, choice as to where and to whom he would sell his labour.

Later my father discovered that what he thought were factories from the air, were in fact terraced houses. While describing this discovery, his tone of voice would always change. Not because he was ashamed of his naïveté, but because it reminded him of factory work: his working environment for most of his working life. Occasionally, he was willing to tell terrible stories of Jamaican citizens' pioneering struggles for opportunities, rights and respect in post-war industrial Britain. But as mentioned above, like many of his generation, he chose not to pass on stories of the hardship, racism and psychological terror that many of the first generation endured. The land was found flowing with less milk and honey than he could have imagined.

However, the story of crossing does not stop here for my father. In comparison to his first journey, his final journey across the Atlantic was as a 'returnee' going home to Jamaica. This journey was quite a contrast to his first visit to England. He returned to Jamaica comparatively wealthy, with a British pension, a house by the sea in Trelawny (a district of Westmorland) and a sense of pride in being able to make it back and help the people he lives amongst and loves. This second story of crossing the Atlantic was a positive experience for my father. As a young man it was a space of hope and as a pensioner it was crossed with thanksgiving. Unlike his African ancestors who made this journey, my father had redeemed the sea; he had crossed over without going under.

My mother came by boat. Her stories are less colourful. However, her main concern about the boat journey was the relationship between stowaways and fee-paying passengers. Her favourite line is, 'We knew a stowaway by the fact that they never had clean shirts.' Coming from a middle-class Jamaican background, class, legality and legitimacy were important to my mother. She came with a more meritocratic world-view:

intelligence and hard work would secure her future. As with my father, her dreams were soon shattered. Encouraged to take the lower ranking nursing qualification despite her intelligence and ability, she became part of the underemployed Jamaicans in 1960s Britain. As Clive Harris and Winston James have shown, underemployment, structural inequality and discrimination were active political policies enacted by Labour and Conservative governments in the 1950s.[8] There was room for Black people at the bottom.

Whereas my father's great ambition was to get out and one day return home, my mother, after three years of retirement with my father in Jamaica, decided to go back to England. She had made a home in England and was not to be hindered by its difficulties and distresses. She had proved that it was possible to remain dignified, raise 'God-fearing' children and consolidate and celebrate in the land flowing with less milk and less honey. She, like my father, redeemed the Atlantic. Her *second* major crossing to the 'mother country' was by choice, not economic necessity – she had survived and thrived in *Babylon*. She also had crossed over without going under.

My journey

However, my journey is qualitatively different compared with the two previous journeys that make my journey possible and necessary. My sense of space and time is very different. I do not travel as an economic unit: that is, whereas my parents travelled for the sake of work – the product of colonialism and capitalism – I travel with the blessing of UK business, as my story was recorded by a television company. Whereas my parents travelled as immigrants and my ancestors as slaves, I travel on a European Community passport – ethnically as part of the Black British community. I am the product of the Jamaican Diaspora in Britain. My parents travelled in hope and expectation of a better life. I cross in order to seek redemption by giving

voice to my ancestors' stories. In my situation the Atlantic represents not just survival or economic betterment, but
psychological, social and political justice. Like many others of
the African diaspora, Paul Gilroy demonstrates, in *The Black
Atlantic*, that the Atlantic space also represents a site of
struggle.[9]

In travelling to Jamaica, my first concern was to find out
whether contemporary Jamaican Christian traditions could
provide me with resources for my analysis. When I arrived in
April 1999, therefore, the first two places that I visited were
churches. I hoped that I would find a redemptive framework
in the Christian traditions of the islands that would support or
challenge my redemptive quest. After all, I was returning 'home',
and 'home' is supposed to have some kind of guidance. What I
am getting at here is the fact that I can think of a number of
friends who found an almost 'supernatural' strength and a
renewed sense of direction upon going to Jamaica for the first
time. One of my friends stood behind a tree and wept in down-
town Kingston because he was so overwhelmed with being in a
Black country where he did not have to 'hide' or wrestle with
the negotiation of his identity, but instead felt a great sense of
acceptance. So for me as a Black Christian searching for a redemptive framework for analysing my name, Jamaican Christianity
seemed like a good place to start. In Kingston and Montego Bay I
found two differing traditions of Jamaican Christian redemption.
These were *Revival* and *Native Baptist* theologies.

Revival

In Kingston I visited a Zion Revivalist Church. Zion Revival
is a derivative of the Great Revival in the early 1860s. It emerged
from the syncretism between the Myal-Obeah (indigenous
African religions) complex and Christianity.[10] Zion Revival in
Jamaica stayed closer to Christianity than other products of the
African/European slave syncretism. However, Revivalism was

more than a religion. As Barry Chevannes has demonstrated, while Revivalism within the context of nineteenth-century colonialism represents a 'complex of beliefs and values', it was also a rejection of the slavemaster's Christianity in the nineteenth century and an endorsement of the African world-views amongst the slaves.[11] Hence, the early story of Revival tells of a counter-hegemonic Christian tradition.

Mount Zion Revival Church on the outskirts of Kingston continues Revival's religious traditions. Throughout the church there is the presence of vegetation, symbolising the life-giving force of God. Also, the spontaneous and antiphonal utterances of the congregation and the expressive physicality in song acknowledge the presence and power of the Spirit's 'moving'. Similarly, the use of poly-rhythmic drumming also invites the presence of 'good' Spirits – as does the consecrated water, white candles and red flags on a table near the altar. Moreover, the wearing of 'African' clothing by the 'father' (minister) and head wraps by both men and women in the congregation also signify the retention of African customs within this Jamaican Christian tradition. The high point of the service came midway through, when the whole congregation 'stepped' in unison around the table at the centre of the altar, rather like the circle dances recorded amongst Africans and Creoles in the Caribbean and North America.[12]

On reflection, what I appreciated about this church was that contemporary Revival reconnects its adherents to an African past, thereby redeeming four hundred years of absence from the continent. In addition, within its context it is a redemptive tradition on several levels. First, contemporary revival is redemptive in that it provides an alternative world-view where the adherents have the spiritual resources to change the course of their lives so as to transcend the limited social expectations of the Jamaican proletariat. As Noel Erskine demonstrates, within the context of neo-colonialism Revivalism offers an important space for resistance, providing poor and underclass

Jamaicans with a place where they are affirmed and empowered despite their lack of resources and status. Second, culturally, Revivalism is pro-Black in that it affirms the African identity and heritage within contemporary Jamaica. Within a post-colonial religious situation where skin colour privilege favours the light skinned elite, Revival with its dark-skinned working poor congregations, most of whom are first- or second-generation migrants from rural regions of the country, indirectly challenges the elitism within the class-ridden Christianity on the Island.[13] Zion Revival reminded me of the importance of saving ourselves as an aspect of redemptive vengeance. Here was a tradition geared towards providing hope and inner strength in the midst of disquiet and hardship. There are, however, several problems and contradictions evident at the place of worship.

Ironically, on the front wall inside of the church hang two portraits of Jesus. He is depicted as a White European male in both. In one picture, containing an image of a crucifixion scene, he has angels at his side. The angels are important because in Revivalism Gabriel and Michael are given powerful status above Christ in the world of the Spirit. As I joined in the worship I wondered, 'How am I to read these images?' Well, on the one hand there is the argument which states that, despite the obvious European influence in the iconography, when the worship and spirituality are placed alongside the European image, Jesus is transformed and 'read' through a powerful African diasporan religious matrix. As a consequence it is possible to argue that in such cases the White Jesus becomes as Black as any African deity. In other words, Revivalism wrests the imperial English Christian Jesus away from his nineteenth-century White supremacist colonial origins and reconstitutes Jesus as the Christ – a servant of the Black 'sufferers' in Jamaica.

On the other hand there is an alternative reading. As I participated in the worship on Sunday till mid-afternoon, I could not stop thinking about the various social, theological and political implications of these divine images. In particular, I thought how affirming and mobilising an effect a *Black* Jesus would have on this proletarian congregation. My conclusion was that Revivalism is unwilling to redeem Blackness in a more explicit way. A more explicit tradition would translate the White Jesus into a Jamaican iconography that represents Jesus and the angels as resembling the majority of the Jamaican people. Such a rereading was not possible because Mount Zion Revival is a 'spiritual' church concerned with addressing 'spiritual' issues that are not seen as being located or related to the concrete socio-political experiences of its adherents. Revival, while reconnecting one to an African world-view and an inherent politics, fails to move beyond the traditional European Churches within the Caribbean.

Sharpe tendencies: the Native Baptist Church

While Zion reminded me of the importance of internal well-being as a dimension of redemptive vengeance, it did not provide me with the necessary inspiration for seeking redress or recompense. However, this was not the case when I visited Montego Bay in search of a more militant religious history. In the centre of one of the districts of Montego Bay I visited the memorial to Sam 'Daddy' Sharpe. It stands within a small square off a busy route through a district of the Bay. The presence of Sharpe tells of another Jamaican Christian tradition forged by slaves.

Creole men and women developed traditions of liberation concerned with overthrowing the brutality of slavery and replacing it with a more just society. From the moment African slaves arrived on the Island they were in rebellion. Some forms were covert, others explicit. The spirit of freedom did not diminish once Christianity replaced African religions as the central religious experience. In fact, it was the potent mixture of African and Christian religions that undergirded the Christian social justice tradition found within the Jamaican Native Baptist Church. One of its most favourite sons is Sam 'Daddy' Sharpe. He was a Baptist deacon from Montego Bay. At the beginning of the 1830s Sharpe developed a Christian faith that demanded as a right freedom for Blacks in Jamaica.

For Sharpe, unlike many of his counterparts in the Anglican clergy, slavery was an abomination in the sight of God. He was also aware that the planters were not going to give up their hold on slavery willingly, and were probably holding back on freedoms granted to slaves from the government in London. Hence, to redeem slavery, civil disobedience was necessary. Sharpe produced an important liberation theology concerned with social change through non-violence. In this case the quest for redemption was married to social disobedience.

Sharpe organised a non-violent mass strike in December 1831. Unfortunately, the plans went amiss and the general strike became a violent national revolt involving 200,000 slaves in rebellion. Even worse for Sharpe, the resistance faltered for a variety of reasons and eventually Sharpe was forced to surrender to the authorities. He felt personally responsible for the thousands of retributive killings carried out by the English regime on the slave population. He was tried and hanged outside the courthouse in Montego Bay in 1832. According to the present minister at Sharpe's current church, Reverend Reid, Sharpe's legacy lives on in two forms.

Sharpe's legacy remains within the Jamaican psyche, in particular in the unwillingness to put up with nonsense. During my visit in the spring of 1999 there were numerous examples of the spirit of Sharpe, particularly the urban protests that occurred when the government increased petrol prices. Rather than remaining silent, masses of urban Jamaicans took to the streets in protest. Eventually the government was forced to back down. Second, according to Revd Reid, the spirit of Sharpe lives on within the history of other militant Jamaicans who transformed Black Nationalism in the twentieth century – people such as

Marcus and Amy Garvey. Marcus Garvey is one of the most important figures in African diasporan history. As the father of twentieth-century Black Nationalism, Garvey organised a global movement concerned with redeeming the diaspora. The spirit of Sharpe lived on in Garvey's mission in the sense that Garvey sought peaceful ways of redeeming the Black people 'captured' in the Western world.

Sharpe provides us with an important insight into redemptive vengeance. First, he promoted a non-violent approach. Although his movement became violent, this was not the primary means of political engagement. Sharpe believed that through peaceful mass protest change was possible. Given the large slave population, he had the upper hand. Second, within this redemptive model there was room for forgiveness and reconciliation. Sharpe was not concerned with annihilating the White population on the Island, or even punishing them for slavery. In fact, many slaves who participated in the uprising warned their masters during the rebellion that disaster was about to strike. They hated the system, but did not see all Whites as worthy of death. In this case a complex notion of justice was also integral to the slaves' quest for freedom.

Both Mount Zion Revival and the Native Baptists provided me with useful Jamaican resources. What these church visits taught me was that there is a need to combine Mount Zion and the Native Baptists as part of a redemptive theology – in particular, I realised the need for a redemptive theology which saves both the self and the society. I now turn to the central concern within my Jamaican journey, to find the origins of my surname.

3. White and Black Beckfords

White Beckfords

In Jamaica I discovered many things about the White Beckford family who had enslaved my African ancestors. The White

Beckford family was the major slave-holding family. At their height they owned 22 plantations and some 1,600 African slaves. The first Beckford began slave-trading and planting as early as the later part of the 1660s.[14] For almost two hundred years, as a result of the huge profits from their plantations in Jamaica, a plethora of Beckford descendants lived lives of luxury and influence in Jamaica and England. Their annual income was between £30,000 and £150,000 per annum back in the nineteenth century! Even at the end of slavery in 1834, the White family received a lump sum for their losses – over £200,000 in compensation. In contrast the Black Beckfords received nothing – no apology was or has ever been given.

My first port of call in search of the White Beckfords was on the west of the Island, the district of Westmorland. One site of strategic importance is the remains of a Beckford plantation house near Roaring River. This site is now a derelict patch of undeveloped land. On one level, the spot bore no resemblance to the eighteenth-century grandeur of the once big house and functioning plantation. Hence, visiting this location as a Black Beckford was not akin to visiting a morgue, although beneath the soil lay stories of toil, depression and possibly hope.

On another level, the site was a symbol of Jamaica's struggle to move away from its colonial past and find a place in the modern Americas. The scarred barren land resonated with the social, emotional and political dereliction that blights aspects of contemporary Jamaican society. The legacy of slavery lives on because today little has changed regarding issues of global inequality and Jamaica's place within it. Independence has *not* brought a land of opportunity and mass prosperity. Instead Jamaica has moved from colonial to multinational commercial exploitation. The main benefactors are no longer English slavers or plantation-owners. Instead, today it is American, Canadian and Japanese big businesses, which carve up among themselves the Island's natural resources, commerce and the tourist industry. Like many small 'developing' countries, Jamaica borrowed heavily from international financiers. Most of the debt has not been repaid and the country is struggling to repay its interest on loans. Over half of Jamaica's GNP services debt! In short, Jamaica has moved from the 'slave chain to the multi-national and IMF (International Monetary Fund) strain'. Despite getting freedom in 1834/8 Jamaicans did not gain any major economic control or advantages. For me, Roaring River is a symbol of past and present economic exploitation.

I also discovered that one of the descendants of the early planting family was Peter Beckford (d. 1711). He was a Governor of Jamaica and his son, also named Peter, was speaker of the Jamaican assembly (d. 1735). The grave of Peter Beckford lies in the cathedral church in Spanish Town. At the altar of this austere Anglican church lie several graves of slave-holding families. This is important symbolism – the Anglican Church, which refused to marry slaves, was willing to bury the slave-holding plantocracy.

Interestingly, visiting Peter Beckford's grave in Spanish Town cathedral was a visit to the location of both ancestors and oppressors. My feelings were varied. How could I feel anything but anger and animosity towards these people? I wondered what my ancestors would have thought of this man who enslaved and tortured them and in some cases sanctioned their deaths. My initial desire was to *spit* on the grave as an act of vengeance for those in the past who could only have dreamed of the freedom that I now have. Indeed, this is what I told the television interviewer. However, alongside the anger was a sense of curiosity. Given the history of rape and sexual exploitation of Black women on Caribbean plantations, was this dead White man also a distant relative? Even so, I felt no sorrow, only curiosity, with no real sense of connection to this White side of the family.

I realised after the visit that being able to identify this location and the contradictions within colonial Christianity was a form of redemption. This became clearer after talking to African-Caribbean people in England who were unaware of these slave facts. I had always known that Black history is a precious commodity that does not always get into the hands or minds of the African-Caribbean diaspora in Britain. Therefore to be able to reveal this past was indeed an act of redemption.

What made me angry was the realisation that Peter Beckford was able to amass a fortune worth millions in wealth and even more in prestige and influence in Jamaica and in England. After his death his sons and relatives were able to reap the rewards of his exploitation. My awareness and understanding of the benefits from slavery became clearer upon returning to England to further trace the White family.

The son of Peter Beckford was Alderman William Beckford (1709–70). He was twice Lord Mayor of London, a Member of Parliament and very wealthy. His statue stands in the Guildhall in London as tribute to his work and support for the City of London in the eighteenth century. His presence in such a prestigious landmark in England is of great consequence. Most important to me is the fact that it reveals London's collusion with and benefit from slavery. Why else would they honour a 'slave Lord' if not to respect his wealth and power? However, it should be noted that despite Alderman Beckford's attempts to recast himself as someone from good stock, his strong Jamaican accent and ungainly manner meant he would never be accepted as one of England's finest. He was still to a great extent an outsider, despite his large fortune and political influence.

The son of Alderman Beckford was the infamous William Thomas Beckford (1760–1844). William Beckford wrote the first Gothic novel (*Vathek*), and rebuilt the family home, Fonthill Abbey (Salisbury), both of which astounded his contemporaries. He also constructed Beckford Tower in Bath.[15]

Beckford Tower still stands today in Bath. Research in England led me to the National Lottery Heritage fund, which had donated £600,000 to restore the tower. While a part of their work is restoration, another dimension is promotion of William

Beckford. Of particular interest and importance to the Tower Trust is his patronage of the arts in Bath.

In one of my discussions at the tower with a representative of the Tower Trust, William Beckford was described as a 'West Indian planter'. This is a really important signifier. The concept of 'planter' has an agricultural feel to it, doesn't it? It implies wholesome yeomen/women in country fields planting to feed the nation. Presenting the Beckford families as 'planters' and patrons, the Trust continues a myth about Beckford, his wealth and its origins. Timothy Mowle[16] has demonstrated in his radical revision of William Beckford that identity politics based on obscuring the truth was 'part and parcel' of Beckford's life. Could it be that the Beckford Tower Trust has fallen into a similar trap, passing Beckford off as something he was not?

The tower, once restored, will be partly a museum dedicated to the Beckford family and their collection of treasure. Part of the plan is to tell the story of this remarkable patron of arts in Bath. The question I had to ask was, 'How does one tell the story of the Beckford family without telling the story of slavery?' The selective appropriation at work here resonates with the type of British history I was taught at school in Coventry. For example, when we were taught about the Industrial Revolution, we were told how the Midlands area was the centre of new processes of production. But we were never told what Eric Williams argued in *Capitalism and Slavery*, namely that the money and wealth generated from the West Indian slave plantations, in great part, provided the capital for the Industrial Revolution. In a similar fashion, representing the life of William Beckford without reference to the Beckford plantations in the Caribbean is also a selective appropriation. I mean, could you talk about the rush to the West of America in the nineteenth century with no mention of the annihilation of the American Indians? This is why it is so important to tell the Black Beckford story also.

Black Beckfords

The starting point for exploring the lives of the Black ancestors began when I visited a slave village. Although not a Beckford
plantation, my visit to the slave village in Saville, in the district
of St Ann's, provided me with some insight into the lives of
Beckford slaves. At Saville lay a site where originally an Arawak
Indian group had settled. The Spanish overran the area and
eventually the site became a slave plantation where Africans
worked and died. As I walked around and thought about the
brutality which took place here, I spoke to the memory of my
ancestors. I thought, 'I can forgive all that has happened –
my faith and my psychological health demands it. However, I
know that I cannot afford to forget all that has taken place here.'

This problematic ethical stance on the nature of forgiveness
is productive because it does *not* make me a victim of the kind
of unfruitful rage which would result in defeat and dejection.
This is the problem I have with one of lines from a 1970s reggae
song by Birmingham-based Steel Pulse. In, 'Ku Klux Klan' one
line reads, 'I'll never forgive, I'll always remember.' To 'never
forgive' makes one a victim locked in time, unable to overcome
and grow by experiencing the power of forgiving. After all, how
can anyone who has experienced the forgiveness of God *not*
forgive with liberality? However, I cannot afford to forget what I
have seen and felt here. Never forgetting means telling this
story so that its significance for the Caribbean diaspora is never
overlooked. However, there is another side to never forgetting.
It is also important to remember that the plantation, despite
its 'concentration camp'-like overtones was also a theatre of
resistance and celebrating overcoming.

What is not shown at Saville is the number of slaves who
downed tools and ran off into the hills and joined the bands of
rebel Maroons (escaped slaves); neither is there evidence of the
numerous personal acts of resistance. As Stella Dadzie has
argued in her analysis of Black women during Jamaican slavery,

recovering the acts of resistance by Black people, particularly by Black women, is vital for redeeming the history through reclamation of its hidden layers.[17] So the fact that, at that moment in time, I was walking around the location and speaking to the memory of my ancestors is another chapter in this story of resistance. There I was, aware of their memory, because they survived and passed their memory on.

I also discovered however, that the Black Beckford story is not as 'African' as I thought. The large part of the Black Beckford story is the tale of the slaves who were forced to work on the White Beckford plantations in one of the cruellest and most desperate episodes of English history. All the same, the Black Beckford families from which I descend were not a homogeneous group. My father told me in the conversation we had after the episode of Alex Haley's *Roots* that his great-grandfather was a White Beckford. In Jamaica, I got the opportunity to check out the accuracy of my father's oral history. There was indeed a White James Beckford in Westmorland who arrived from St Elizabeth some time in the 1870s. He married – or had children with – a Black woman, one of whom was Uziah Beckford. One of Uziah's sons was John, and one of John's many children was my father, Leonard Beckford. Leonard Seymour Beckford was part of the *Windrush* generation, arriving in Britain in the 1950s as a 'West Indian' migrant. He settled in the Midlands (Coventry) where he worked in the building trade.

In Westmorland I was able to interrogate my father and some of his relatives about their feelings towards the White folk in the family. Unlike me, my father and his peers were very impressed with the White roots in their ancestry. Their White ancestor was a 'badge of honour'. As I sat and talked to them I thought of how their dark skins were redeemed by this White heritage. Like the adherents at Mount Zion Revival Church, this small group of Black Beckfords were not willing to let go of or severely critique their commitment to Whiteness. Their post-colonial racial reasoning led them to perceive their White ancestry as something positive. But this was not the full picture. They were also proud 'Jamaican' people who appreciated all that they as Black people had achieved. There was no prouder Jamaican than my father. So as well as being proud of their White heritage they were also proud of the present reality of being Black in Jamaica. They were 'at home' holding both traditions together without any identifiable tension. As Garth and Karen Baker-Fletcher have suggested, African diasporan communities often embrace 'diunital' realities where opposing concepts or relations are held together without contradiction or tension.[18] My father's generation had found a way to redeem their oppressors, by embracing their White ancestors and placing them with their Black ancestors.

The Black Beckford narrative as understood by my father and his relatives has significance for identity formation in Black Britain today. My father's history shows me that my identity is not fixed, but constantly 'on the move'. The motto on the Jamaican coat of arms, 'Out of many one people', should really read, 'Out of many have developed a hybrid and complex people'! Therefore my identity as an 'African-Caribbean' man in Britain must be understood as a fluid identity and not a fixed one. In terms of contemporary Britain, reclaiming this hybrid identity has the potential to challenge fixed or essentialist notions of Black identity by revealing and *revelling* in the history of cultural diversity, which emerges through the cultural interfaces of the past. It is a shame that there are strong moves to deny this complex history and attempt to fix or 'police' Blackness. It is almost as though the complex of African and European cultures that constitutes African-Caribbean identity has been lost in Britain. As Ayse Caglar warns, hyphenated identities such as African-Caribbean run the risk of re-creating essentialist identities.[19]

Three hundred lashes and life imprisonment

Upon returning to England, I searched through records of the Black family for any important areas left out by the Jamaican Beckfords. To my surprise, I discovered an important hidden narrative within the Black Beckford family at the Public Record Office in London. This story concerns one 'Robert Beckford', a slave from Trelawny born around 1800. Bearing my name some one hundred and seventy years before my birth, this Robert Beckford was probably a Christian who, like Sam Sharpe, believed in emancipation. The slave Robert Beckford was willing to engage in the 1831 civil disobedience to gain his freedom as part of the Baptist rebellion. Like the rebellion's architect, Sam Sharpe, Robert Beckford was punished when the rebellion failed in 1832. He received 300 lashes and life imprisonment for his part in the uprising. Little is known of what happened to him after the rebellion. But this narrative is of fundamental importance in my quest to redeem my name.

Robert Beckford the slave offers an alternative point of focus in the quest for redemption. Here lies an example of a Black Beckford identity that was concerned with outright liberation. In this case, rather than the surname being associated with White domination, it is overturned to become a signifier of Black Christian rebellion. On one level this Robert Beckford symbolises the early quest for a political theology within my 'very loose' family history. With this important discovery, the final question I want to address is whether the discovery of a redemptive Black male Beckford is sufficient grounds for retaining my surname in contemporary Britain? There are two questions that need to be answered. First, how do I redeem the White family and, second, what do I do with the name?

Redeeming the family and redeeming the name

How do I redeem the White family? For me, a redemptive vengeance applied to this situation has several facets. First, redeeming this history means forgiveness in the present, embracing the White Beckfords today and giving them room for repentance and restitution. However, this process is not an easy one, as such forgiveness guided by love is a gift from God. What I am saying is that this is where supernatural realities take over – I forgive because my faith demands it and because it is the right thing to do, despite the pain, anger and rage I feel as a descendant of slavery.

The meeting of Black and White Beckfords is a paradigm of redemption. For me this process has begun. I was able to meet John Beckford, a descendant of the White Beckford dynasty in Britain, as part of the programme for Channel 4. In my initial meeting my primary concern was to address the issue of reparation. For John the answer lay in the present. Teaching the next generation to treat all people with equality and equity can redeem the history. However, this was not enough for me. For me, as shown in my analysis of eschatology in Chapter 2, three-dimensional time is crucial here – the past, the present and the future are intimately related. Therefore it is impossible to talk about a just future without addressing the atrocities of the past. As I argued in 'Forgive and forget' in *Jesus is Dread*, Black folks should forgive, but we should not forget while the injustice from the past continues. Hence to have dialogue between the families today would go some way on an interpersonal level to redeem the past. However, such an act must involve an exploration of reparations. In short, redeeming the White family means that I will work with the descendant of the people who enslaved my ancestors in order to heal the memory and ensure that the past is not repeated through ignorance.

Second, redeeming the White family also means ensuring that the bigger and broader story about the Beckford family is told. This means ensuring that the Beckford Tower Trust must not focus on the White Beckford family without telling the story of the Black Beckford family. Hence the act of restoration should involve the Black Beckfords also. We are here because they were there: our family histories are irrefutably intertwined. What this means for me is that as well as portraying the 'romantic' and 'eccentric' life of the White Beckfords, biographers must also deal with their 'slaving' in the Caribbean. The intentions at present are to portray the White family as rich, quirky and eccentric collectors of fine art. What should also be made clear is that this family gained its wealth from its involvement with crimes against humanity. Their wealth came from brutal treatment of African slaves in one of the worst episodes of English history.

Third, redeeming this history must also involve reparations. For example, one creative outcome from the restoration of the Beckford Tower and other buildings could be that a percentage of any profits made from the tower should be sent back to Jamaica. As mentioned in the introduction, an integral dimension of redemption is reparation. Although the tower is not set to be a great money-spinner, reparation would be a powerful symbolic gesture. On one level it would tell the nation that justice in the present and future is built upon repentance. On another level it would be an important educative tool, reminding all of us what human beings are capable of doing to one another, and the danger inherent in closing the eyes to aspects of history and culture.

Redeeming the name

Regarding the second question, there are those in my family who thought that it was not necessary to be concerned with this redeeming the family name. The main argument within this camp was historical. The history of slavery and colonialism happened a long time ago and, moreover, the White Beckfords who enslaved our ancestors are now dead and buried. I would find this school of thought more compelling if the ripples from slavery, that is, contemporary English racism, were not all so evident in contemporary Britain. The womanist theologian Kelly Brown Douglas's analysis of Black sexuality resonates with my concerns here. Douglas shows that the cheapening of Black life in the past is inextricably linked to the treatment of Black bodies in the present.[20] Therefore exploring the politics and culture associated with my family name has significance for Black culture and politics today.

After my visit to Jamaica, initially, I felt uncomfortable, having visited the plantations where my ancestors worked, and seen the 'palaces' built by their oppressors. It became clear that my surname truly signified oppression in the past. Despite their proud Jamaican heritage, even the positive affirmation provided by my Black relatives in Jamaica failed to convince me fully that the name was redeemable. Their analysis works well in post-colonial Jamaica, where names tell important stories and identify family/kinfolk connections on the Island. But their post-colonial world is not the one in which I currently live. I do not live in Jamaica. If I were living there then my identity politics would be very different. This process of creating and re-constructing cultural identity in response to a given social situation is an example of a situational ethnicity – what Claire Alexander calls the art of being Black.[21]

The most positive expression of my surname was located in the discovery of a slave called Robert Beckford who was a part of the Christian-led rebellion of 1831. In this case the Beck-ford name signifies positive resistance to White oppression. However, if I am to take seriously the 'Sharpe' tendencies in Jamaican culture, then I must ask whether this discovery is sufficient to invigorate the surname for me today. What can I do with this surname in order to redeem it? There are at least two options. The first involves changing the surname altogether; the second involves altering it in some degree. An example of the first tradition is found in the replacement of European slave names with African names.

Many people I know who have become cognisant of this history have opted for African names. The idea here is that one bypasses slave history and returns to an African identity. This has always been a popular option amongst the African diaspora; in particular, the cultural nationalists of the 1960s viewed name changes as a resurrection experience. The Negro died and the reclaimed African arose with a new name. For example, in *Afrocentricity*, Molefi Kete Asante connects choosing an African name with a rise in Afrocentric consciousness.[22] While this naming process reconnects Black people with our African origins, it does not always do justice to the journey that has shaped us, because it does not want to learn from it.

In my case, removing the Beckford name and taking an African name would remove the history and memory of the name. To do this would be akin to the restoration of Rose Hall in Montego Bay. Rose Hall is a redeveloped 'great house' from the days of slavery. Here thousands of dollars have been spent on improvements to the house and grounds near the bay. It is a major tourist attraction. There is, however, no evidence that slaves once roamed the house, cut sugar cane on the lawns or slept in the doorways and under the stairs. Neither is there any sign that slaves resisted, celebrated and challenged slavery. Rose Hall is a sanitised history of the 'great house' near the bay. Likewise to remove the Beckford name and replace it with an African name, despite the liberative dimensions of such an act, would also be an act of sanitising the past and re-establishing my identity by taking a name from the language of my unknown forebears. This is one of the problems of Afrocentric worldviews. We often deny the liberative aspects of the journey that has shaped who we are.

An example of the second option is found in the change of surnames in the African diaspora. For example, there are

Jamaicans who choose to spell their surname backwards. This inversion designates the hidden history of Africans that lies beneath the history and experience associated with the slave name. In this case 'Beckford' would become 'Drofkceb'. I guess you have to have a name that sounds or looks good when inverted for it really to work here! Another approach is found in the way in which the Black British feminist Helen Charles chooses to identify herself. Charles is presented in brackets and with a lower-case 'c'. Helen Charles becomes Helen (charles). This process identifies the surname as an aberration and of lesser significance than the forename given by her parents. Once again, the lower-case 'c' signifies its status as 'less than' and the enclosure within brackets symbolises what is unknown or hidden beneath this name. This symbolism ensures that the memory is not forgotten. In addition it presents a lived tension, an internal dialectic. I tried this approach for a while but got fed up with having to explain it every time I wrote my name. Even so the bracketing approach has value because it separates our forename from our surname. This approach would have been my first choice if I had not discovered the slave named 'Robert Beckford'. This discovery provided me with another alternative.

One of my favourite Black feminist writers, bell hooks, provides a model for redeeming my family name. bell hook's real name is Gloria Watkins. She writes in the name of her grandmother, Bell Hooks, but spells the name without capitals. Writing with someone else's name may happen for a variety of reasons, but here it is not to obscure the real writer. In contrast, here the traditional pseudonym is turned on its head, because the purpose is to promote the adopted name, not to obscure her real name. By writing with her grandmother's name, Watkins is giving voice to a Black woman who, like many of her generation, was silenced by the race, class and gender politics of nineteenth- and early twentieth-century USA. Could this process work for me?

Finding the slave Robert Beckford provides me with a

similar avenue of expression. On this occasion, however, there is no need for a literal name change, although there *is* a change in orientation. By retaining the name, I can make a connection between my slave ancestor and myself. In this sense, retaining the name with these implications is a powerful act of redemption. This is because the slave name on this occasion is a symbol of Christian resistance to racism. 'Beckford' the 'slave name' is overturned so as to represent a motif for overcoming. However, as I said at the beginning, this journey is on a trajectory – after my visit to West Africa, I may not feel the same way about this name.

4.
Miseducation: Lauryn Hill and redemptive vengeance

Introduction

As mentioned in Chapter 2, 'redemptive vengeance' is concerned with saving ourselves, that is, calling for a return to the source, or repentance. Repentance creates an environment for change where forgiveness and restitution are made possible. As a consequence new beginnings are achievable – including meaningful dialogue and the redemption of those responsible for 'downpression'. In the previous chapter I showed how redemptive vengeance was mobilised on a personal level in attempts to redeem my slave name. As mentioned in the introduction to this book, for several reasons I am concerned with a theological engagement with Black popular culture. Therefore it makes sense to identify ways in which redemptive vengeance as a theological reality can engage with Black popular culture.

Black popular culture is a resource for doing Black theology. As Theo Smith advocates, a pharmacopoeic[1] appraisal of culture enables us to look for what provides both healing and harm in Black cultures. Redemptive vengeance is concerned with identifying life-giving and life-sustaining dimensions of Black expressive cultures; in particular, redemptive vengeance explores cultural forms that explore forgiveness, restitution, reconciliation and love. Central to redemptive vengeance is the quest for ways in which expressive culture can be used to enable redemption both inside and outside of Black communities. In this chapter I want to engage in a dialogue between redemptive vengeance and aspects of hip-hop culture.

Hip-hop cultures are important for three reasons. The first reason is that no other Black cultural form has been as influential in Black Atlantic cultures in the last 21 years. Second, this 'black noise' emerging from Black urban life-settings is fecund with themes, ideas and motifs relevant to redemptive vengeance. This leads to the third point. A part of exploring redemptive vengeance in hip-hop is to explore miseducation – the ways in which hip-hop artists fail to produce meaningful redemption.

In order to demonstrate redemptive vengeance within aspects of hip-hop I want to engage in a theomusicological[2] analysis, identifying the meaning of redemptive vengeance in hip-hop. First, I will explore dimensions and aspects of redemptive vengeance in the historical origins of hip-hop. After this, I will explore redemptive vengeance in the work of the hip-hop artist Lauryn Hill.

1. Origins of hip-hop and redemptive vengeance

The origins of hip-hop, when analysed from the perspective of redemptive vengeance, reveal significant liberative themes in the origins of the genre. Hip-hop history is important because liberation theologies have long identified historical experiences as a source of divine revelation. In Black liberation theology, critical interrogation of this perspective has led to a broader analysis of Black history that incorporates both the heroic and the grotesque as sites of God's activity. In sum, Black theologians acknowledge that one can learn from both that which is good and that which is bad in Black history.

On a general note, hip-hop is part of a continuing experience of Black music as Chuck D of Public Enemy states: 'Hip-hop is just Black people's creativity, and we've always been creative people. So it's just a term for the last twenty-five years.' On a more specific note, hip-hop, like all Black popular music, emerges from distinct yet complex historical contexts and cannot easily be severed from the socio-historic and socio-political moment in which it occurs. The backdrop to the emergence of this sound was a complex interplay of social and economic forces in New York in the 1960s. New York's South Bronx, the birthplace of hip-hop, was in the grip of post-industrial decline, which had devastating effects on Black and Hispanic communities.[3] Faced with urban decay and fragile economic opportunities:

> North American blacks, Jamaicans, Puerto Ricans, and other Caribbean people with roots in other postcolonial contexts reshaped their cultural identities and expressions in a hostile, technologically sophisticated, multiethnic, urban terrain.[4]

Hip-hop culture was one of the responses to de-industrialisation. Through the creation of new music, dance and art, African Americans, Caribbean migrants and Hispanic youth were able to create an alternative identity deeply connected to the local environment.

Unfortunately, mainly male researchers and historians have negated the roles of women in the origins of hip-hop. As a consequence, the origins are represented as an all-male affair. Likewise the Caribbean dimension of the early origins is also overlooked. However, as Ulf Poschardt has shown, hip-hop has distinctively Jamaican roots.[5] The Jamaican sound system DJs of the 1960s developed the dub version of records – reducing a piece to the drum and bass. Furthermore, they developed a lyrical style or 'toasting' that was a rhythmic form of talking over the dub track. Like many other musical forms this genre was transported and reworked as Caribbean migrants entered the North American East Coast.

In this brief theomusicological analysis, I want to interrogate three traditions at the heart of the origins of hip-hop from the perspective of redemptive vengeance. These are (1) innovation, (2) social organisation and (3) hermeneutics of inclusion. What I want to suggest is that the origins of hip-hop provide us with a Black cultural creativity, central to redemptive vengeance.

Innovation

To redeem a situation requires ingenuity and intelligence. Ingenuity provides resourcefulness necessary for addressing situations of rage, inequality and oppression. Likewise, creativity enables marginalised people to find ways to turn around or stir up so as to redeem the current situation. Hence, ingenuity and creativity are essential to redemptive vengeance. In Black Britain Black ingenuity is rarely acknowledged and affirmed. Usually it is copied, exploited and de-contextualised so that that traditions, ideas and systems of liberation devised in Black spaces are made to look as though they could never have come from Black people. One only has to look at the widespread use of Black language or 'Black twang' beyond Black communities to find a living example of this process. Ingenuity and creativity lie at the heart of the birth of hip-hop.

Black communities in 1960s America lived in a contradictory space. On the one hand, Black Nationalism and the Civil Rights Movement were promising a better tomorrow through Black love and self-sufficiency. On the other hand, many Black communities were still blighted by structural unemployment and underemployment, vicious racism and internecine warfare between gangs. It was into this situation that Clive Campbell, a Jamaican teenager, migrated to New York in 1967. After accepting an invitation to play at a friend's party, Campbell became known as 'Kool DJ Herc', offering his musical services at block parties and thereby presenting an alternative space for celebration, innovation and creativity within the Bronx district of New York. By 1969 Campbell was DJ-ing at local parties in the Bronx. Kool Herc is considered the godfather of hip-hop.[6] His claim to fame is the development of the breakbeat.

Taking the cue from the dub version of reggae in Jamaica, Herc realised that by continually playing breaks (the climactic instrumental section of a record) on his 'prehistoric' Gerald turntables and a preamp with two mixer buttons, he could keep the dancers and the party dancing. What Herc termed the 'merry-go-round' became the basis of hip-hop music. As Afrika Bambaataa states, 'He just kept that being going.'[7] Like the music, the dancing was re-coded, introducing new elements. As Stuart Hall has shown, the body as 'canvas' is strategic in the creation of Black popular cultures.[8] Hence, a whole discipline of dancing by Breakdancers or B-boys and B-girls evolved from the party-goers who waited for his breaks to parade their *locking* and *popping* to them. With Herc, the DJ became a musician, deconstructing in order to interpret and reconstruct.

Barbados born Joseph Sadler, aka Grandmaster Flash, took the hip-hop genre further. Raised in the Bronx and influenced by the turntable dynamics of Kool Herc, Flash set about adding to the turntable 'science'. Unlike Herc, Sadler's background in electronics enabled him to add technological innovations to mixing. As a result Grandmaster Flash is credited with several innovations. First, he is given the credit for 'punch phrasing' – playing a breakbeat together with the instrumentation of another piece – and 'backspinning' – pulling back a break without losing the beats. Second, Flash perfected 'scratching' – adding the rhythmic use of the record needle to keep the groove. While there has always been some controversy over who invented scratching, it is now acknowledged that while Flash popularised 'scratching', it was his one-time helper Grand Wizard Theodore (Theodore Livingstone) who was the first to discover the art.[9] In addition to these innovations, Flash was also responsible for technological advances such as 'cueing' and the development of the beatbox – the use of an electronic drum machine to add extra percussion to the mix.[10]

What I want to suggest is that, while I am not trying to romanticise the history of hip-hop, Herc and Flash were responsible for producing innovative and creative musical styles that helped to offer a 'way out' of a depressing situation for many youths. Technically their musical style placed the DJ in the position of a conjurer – creating new music. Hence, innovation was at the heart of the origins of hip-hop. Redemptive vengeance embraces ingenuity as a tool in the quest for redemption. However, innovation needs a social movement to carry it along. This is why Afrika Bambaataa's explicit social and political grounding for the new music form is of great importance.

Social organisation

Redemptive vengeance also requires a social or political focus in order to challenge and transform existing structures. That is, to save Black people we need to introduce new ways of being. Despite its shortcomings from a feminist or Afrocentric viewpoint, at the outset of hip-hop culture the Zulu Nation attempted to put into action a social plan to redeem Black and Latino youths.

As suggested above, hip-hop block parties provided an important diversion away from the social decay of the Bronx in the 70s. According to Nelson George, of particular importance was the role of Black women in encouraging their men away from gangs and into more productive and wholesome pursuits.[11] The prime mover in the development of transition of the gang-members into hip-hoppers was Afrika Bambaataa.

Bambaataa loved the music. His interest in mixing and scratching was no less keen than that of Herc or Flash. Moreover, Bambaataa's musical range was wider and freakier – he would mix music from Motown to Hare Krishna! He listened to beats without prejudice. Bambaataa's musical eclecticism was married to a love and determination to empower Black people.

Growing up in the late 60s in New York, Bambaataa was influenced by Black Nationalist thought and activism. He had learned to organise and motivate his peers as a gang leader. These skills became increasingly relevant when in 1975, after witnessing the murder of a friend, Bambaataa sought an alternative to gang life and found salvation in hip-hop – a phrase he claims to have coined.[12] While still in high school in 1975 he formed 'The Organisation', which eventually became the 'Zulu Nation', and he took the name Bambaataa, from a nineteenth-century Zulu chief. As shown in the previous chapter, name changes are of great social and political significance in African diasporan communities.

The aims of the Zulu Nation were to add consciousness and social critique to hip-hop. Through a collection of DJs, graffiti artists and breakers both Black and Hispanic, the Zulu Nation set about offering a musical-political-spiritual alternative to gangs, crime and drugs. The International Zulu Nation lives on today; its aims identify the commitment to social organisation at the heart of a core sector of the origins of hip-hop:

> The Universal Zulu Nation started in the borough of the Bronx, New York by Afrika Bambaataa in 1973. It was the idea of Afrika Bambaataa to use music to spread the message of the Universal Zulu Nation. He knew that music crossed all barriers. So with the birth of Hip-Hop culture, Afrika Bambaataa and members of Soulsonic Force, Shango, Rock Steady Crew, Grand Mixer D.S.T, Fab 5 Freddy, Phase 2, Futura 2000, and Dondi started to travel throughout Europe and other countries to bring the Hip-Hop culture to the world. The Universal Zulu Nation has hundreds of chapters throughout the world whose members believe in Knowledge, Wisdom, Understanding, Freedom, Justice, and Equality. Its members come from many races, different religions, cultures, and countries. Zulu Nation members discourage

divisions and foresee peace and unity on this planet with all races! Without these, we face all social, economic, physical, and spiritual destruction. In the Universal Zulu Nation there are DJs, Rappers, Dancers, Graffiti (Aerosol) Artists, Writers, Lawyers, Teachers, Lecturers, Producers, Photographers, and Executives. They believe that the key to our survival is creating a Network that caters to the need of its members and communities around the world. There are many programs within the Universal Zulu Nation that deal with community services and social awareness programs. Other programs that we offer within the Universal Zulu Nation include: Music Business Awareness, Cultural Exchange, Youth Physical Fitness, Internet training and awareness, Mentor Programs, Community Mediation (Conflict Resolving).[13]

So as well as innovation, social organisation, despite its limitations in terms of inclusivity and gender roles, was also an important feature at the heart of the origins of hip-hop.

Hermeneutics of inclusion

Finally, ingenuity and social organisation were in dialogue with the new musical form being developed. What I want to argue is that a *hermeneutics of inclusion* emerged from the music. 'Hermeneutics of inclusion' describes a process of interpreting the world so as to include the 'Other' within one's redemptive plan rather than exclude them from it. People of the African diaspora have historically experienced the contrary, that is, the *hermeneutics of exclusion*, whereby we have been left out of charters, declarations and the political plans of the rich, powerful and mostly White in the West. The hermeneutics of inclusion is important for redemptive vengeance because as an active force its final goal is love – the process of bringing people together in a new relationship as a result of forgiveness, restitution and reconciliation. What I want to show in brief is that the turntable science was symbolic of new social relationships being formed. In particular there was a hermeneutic of inclusion within the process of the *break* and the *mix*.

First, the break offers us an important resource. The break – the climactic instrumental section of a record – is a sophisticated space where past and present are combined to produce a new sound. There is both rupture and continuity. However, as Paul Gilroy argues, the break goes beyond the turntable:

> The centrality of the break . . . the aesthetic rules which govern it are premised on a dialectic of rescuing appropriation and recombination which creates special pleasures and is not limited to the technological complex in which it originated.[14]

What I want to suggest is that the break provides an important *conceptual space*. Regarding conceptual space, the break is concerned with social inclusivity because the turntable provides a new way of understanding 'tradition'. Break after break combined and reconfigured reveals how it is possible to stand within a (musical) tradition, but not limited by it. For example, as mentioned above, Bambaataa showed how one can draw from a vast range of musical forms to create a new musical mix on the record deck where past and present are woven together to create a new tradition and a new cultural identity. This kind of 'changing-same' has implications beyond the turntable. In particular, new identities are forged through the break, that is, the break provides a window on the past that is cut into the present so as to constitute a new mix – in this case the inclusive politics exemplified in the Zulu Nation.

Second, inclusion was practised and perfected conceptually in the mix. The mixing process enabled 'breaks' and 'samples' from a plethora of cultural musical traditions to be mixed into the Black R & B in the Bronx. Such layering of sounds upon sounds might also be considered a process of identity formation.

That is, Black and Latino youths were able to develop an approach to multiculturalism through a deconstruction (taking apart musical compositions) and reconstruction (putting them back together in a new format for popular consumption). The mix also represents *an interpretive skill* – providing the raw material for a Black-based inclusivity.

Hence, at the heart of hip-hop were *innovation* and *social organisation* and *a hermeneutics of inclusion*. All of these themes, I have argued, are relevant to redemptive vengeance. Next I want to focus on *rap* as a pretext for exploring the music and lyrics of Lauryn Hill.

2. Rap

Although hip-hop culture was a mixture of radical urban art forms from rap to graffiti artists, it has been rap that has been the main conduit of hip-hop culture. I want to explore redemptive vengeance through three areas of rap. These are *personal experience, orality and technology* and finally *diversity.*

First, rappers utilise personal experience: they are narrators observing and telling stories from their perspective. These Afro-diasporic oral traditions, while subjective, are still able to convey universal appeal, which enables their messages, codes and themes to go beyond the boundaries of Black communities. Rap sells as well in White suburbs as in multicultural urban areas. Personal experience is a hotly contested arena. Of great concern is the politics of authenticity, that is, honesty and accountability for one's lyrics. On the one hand, the politics of authenticity are concerned with 'keeping it real', that is, telling it like it is. Usually this means maintaining what Garth Baker-Fletcher calls a 'ghettocentric' message, glorifying Black male outlaw culture. On the other hand the politics of authenticity are concerned with remaining true to the 'cause'. Whether it is Black liberation, community organisation or self-love, the opposite of 'keeping it real' is contradiction, duplicity or neglect – which is being 'fake'.

From the perspective of redemptive vengeance, the use of personal experience as the criterion of meaning is affirmed. As mentioned in Chapter 1, Black theology prioritises Black experience in the quest for theological questions emerging from Black life-settings. It is viewed as an important tool for bringing to the surface issues and concerns of Black people that are generally neglected in the wider society. Personal experience, however, is not sacrosanct – it must be scrutinised and subjected to criticism. This is particularly important when exploring the experiences, however, described in gangsta or sexual play rap.

Second, rap's Afrodiasporic oral traditions are intimately related to technologised music. In short, the technology informs the rap and the rap informs the technology. As was the case with my analysis of the mix and the break, hip-hop produces its own theory. Likewise the mutual dialogue occurring between music beats, samples and raps produces theory. From the perspective of redemptive vengeance, Trishia Rose's analysis of the lyrics–technology interface is significant. Rose located a *theory of resistance* within the dialogue between rapper and technology; I quote her at length:

> Rappers layer meaning by using the same words to a
> variety of actions and objects: they call out to the DJ to
> 'lay down a beat', which is expected to be interpreted,
> ruptured. DJs layer sound literally one on top of the other,
> creating a dialogue between sampled sound and words.
> What is the significance of flow, layering and rupture as
> demonstrated on the body and in hip-hop's lyrical, musical
> and visual works? Interpreting these concepts
> theoretically, one can argue that they create and sustain
> rhythmic motion, continuity, and circularity via flow;
> accumulate, reinforce, and embellish this continuity
> through layering; and manage threats to these narratives

by building in ruptures that highlight the continuity as it momentarily challenges it. These effects at the level of style and aesthetics suggest affirmative ways in which profound social dislocation and rupture can be managed and perhaps contested in the cultural arena. Let us imagine these hip-hop principles as a blueprint for social resistance and affirmation: create sustaining narratives, accumulate them, layer, embellish, and transform them. However, be also prepared for rupture, find pleasure in it, in fact, *plan* on social rupture. When these ruptures occur, use them in creative ways that will prepare you for a future in which survival will demand a sudden shift in ground tactics.[15]

Third, as well as drawing on personal experience and the oral-technological interface, rap is not a homogeneous art form. There are several types within the genre. Ethicist Garth Baker-Fletcher has identified five interrelated types of rap music, which are useful to this study.[16] To begin with, there is *gangsta rap*. Gangsta rap is concerned with articulating ghettocentric realities. In short, as mentioned above, the politics of authenticity demand that rappers 'keep it real', so that rap represents the 'outlaw' lifestyles of African Americans. Gangsta rap is mediated through the 'hyperreal' – confusing the boundaries between fact and fiction.[17] Through ultra-masculine personas gangsta rappers articulate views on sex, violence and other aspects of American culture. As is the case with all forms within this genre, gangsta rap is not a homogeneous form. For example, while some gangsta rappers engage in a political critique (the early work of Ice Cube) others reject Black politics and adopt an ambivalent or anti-political perspective (Dr Dre).

There have been very few women who might be considered gangsta-rappers. The machismo within this form does not easily lend itself to female participation. Even so, H.W.A. (Hoez With Attitude) represented a female response to the male domination of gangsta rap.[18] Gangsta rap is infamous for its gun-toting, violent and misogynistic lyrics, much of which is antithetical to the cause of redemptive vengeance. Even so, Garth Baker-Fletcher argues that, while the Black Church might have serious objections to this genre, there is also much to be learned from it. In particular, the ghettocentricity reminds Christians of the necessity of ensuring our message gets a hearing on the 'streets'. Ghettocentricity demands a contextual theology that resonates with the existential questions represented in 'thug life'. For example, the ethicist Anthony Pinn has demonstrated the importance of drawing out, analysing and applying the social critique within this genre.[19] Going one step further, Michael Eric Dyson suggests that Black Christians can learn from the gangsta Afro nationalism – the attempt to combine street savvy with neo-Black Nationalist politics.[20] In Chapter 5, I take these issues on board in the quest for doing theology with Black offenders.

Then there is *revolutionary rap*. Revolutionary rap is alternatively known as progressive rap. It is an African-centred challenge to power structures. Revolutionary rap takes a particular ontological stance.[21] In this case it is a call for Black men and women to engage in resistance through social and cultural criticism, political action and historical excavation. Dead Prez stands as an example of early twenty-first-century revolutionary rap.[22] In the UK context, Black Radical is an example of progressive rap. *Raptivists* (rap activists) in female circles uplift Black women and offer practical and Afrocentric solutions to Black problems. However, not all raptivists adopt the same politics. Take, for example, the work of Erykah Badu. Badu adopts a loose Afrocentrism and is more concerned with individual ethics and aesthetics, all of which suggests an alternative expression of progressive rap. What is important here is the development of what Cornel West calls 'the new cultural politics of difference'. According to West:

> The new cultural politics of difference are neither simply oppositional in contesting the mainstream for inclusion,

nor transgressive in the avant-gardist sense of shocking conventional bourgeois audiences. Rather, they are distinct articulations of talented contributors to culture who desire to align themselves with demoralized, demobilized and disorganized people in order to empower and enable social action and if possible, to enlist collective insurgency for the expansion of freedom, democracy, and individuality.[23]

From the perspective of redemptive vengeance, revolutionary rap offers a potent critique of the Black Church. The Black Church is challenged to show its pro-Black credentials by organising and developing programmes, attitudes and action that actively liberate Black people from all that ravages Black life. Furthermore, the embrace of the Nation of Islam by many raptivists suggests that the Christian Church is not seen as a vehicle for revolutionary change. This may be one of the reasons for the entry of gangsta gospel bands into the gangsta genre. While utilising similar musical techniques gospel artists aim to challenge the violence, misogyny and hopelessness evident in much of the gangsta rap tradition. Gospel gangsta artists such as Gospel Gangstas also hope to reorientate the Black Church towards a streetwise social ministry.

Next, there is *sexual-play* rap, which focuses on sexual pleasure. Sexual-play rappers base their success on selling sex. It is important to remember that sexual-play lyrics are constructed within a highly gendered society characterised by sexism and misogyny. In contemporary rap, good examples of sexual-play rap are 'soft porn rappers' Foxy Brown and Lil' Kim. Whereas revolutionary rap attempts to explore the problems of everyday life of Black women, sexual-play rap explores male and female sexual roles, designer clothes, big mansions and fast cars. Garth Baker-Fletcher suggests that while Black Christians may object to the abuse of sex and the degradation of women's bodies in aspects of sexual-play rap, they must take seriously the aspects of sexual play that focus on the celebration of the body. In short, a positive human sexuality must affirm 'our God-given sensuality'.[24] On this level, sexual-play rap reminds the Church of the importance of connecting spirituality with sexuality in a constructive and positive way.

The penultimate form is *crossover rap*, which is generally apolitical and non-threatening. For example, the work of Will Smith, Puff Daddy and TLC and are good examples of crossover rap. In the UK context, Richard Blackwood and Monie Love are good examples. Crossover rap aims to take a 'status rap' to the masses. Status rap is concerned with 'boasts' and 'dissing'. Because of its distance from the hard-core themes in gangsta and revolutionary rap, crossover artists are often accused by purists of having 'sold out'. And finally there is *inspirational rap*, which is directed at inspiring young people into more positive directions. Baker-Fletcher suggests that most Christian rappers can be placed within this category.

Above, I have outlined some of the redemptive themes that emerged from aspects of hip-hop culture. I have shown that redemptive vengeance can be found in parts of the origins of hip-hop. I have also reviewed the wide variety of genres within hip-hop's most celebrated form, that is, rap. In particular, I have 'hinted' that not all of these forms are emancipatory, neither are they devoid of revolutionary aspirations. This leads me to a diametrically opposed analysis of technologised musical forms.

It would be wrong to present hip-hop, as a form of techno-logical music, as inherently redemptive. On the contrary, there is within hip-hop an anti-redemptive tradition, that is, a tradition of music and lyrics concerned with de-contextualisation and dissociation from socio-political concerns. A classic review of the anti-redemptive tradition in Black music in general and rap in particular is found in a text by Kodwo Eshun, the Black British 'concept engineer' (writer/cultural critic/social analyst), who has argued that there is at least a 30-year tradition of anti-redemptive technologised music within Black popular music. Brief analyses of his ideas are necessary to refocus my assumptions about hip-hop.

3. Against redemption: *More Brilliant than the Sun: Adventures in Sonic Fiction*

In *More Brilliant than the Sun: Adventures in Sonic Fiction*, Kodwo Eshun explores images of the future in Black music – that is, he is concerned with how Black musicians envisage the future of the world, society and culture in their music. Eshun begins this analysis with the 60s African-American techno pioneer, Sun Ra, and concludes with the contemporary Black British drum and bass experts, 4 Hero. Eshun shows that whereas most interpretations of Black music (such as mine above) explore the historical development of Black music as though there is a gradual progression, in contrast he himself is concerned with the discontinuity and rupture. As a result he is able to explore themes such as anti-humanitarianism, and anti-redemptive traditions in Black music.

According to Eshun, post-soul (technologised music that followed soul music) is indifferent towards the plight of humanity and not at all concerned with Black redemption. The reason for this is that many of these musicians have unmasked Black redemption as a kind of post-slave consciousness created in slave and post-slave 'concentration camps' of the West and regulated by White power structures.

The strands of post-structuralism in Eshun have a theological counterpart. As Victor Anderson has argued, Black theologians would do well to explore the problematic and the grotesque in Black life also.[25] Charting a course from 1968 to

1975, Eshun identifies several moments in Black music that explain his thesis.

Eshun begins with the Afrodelic space programme – musicians who combine their creative genius with music machine technology – and includes aspects of Miles Davis, Herbie Hancock and Sun Ra. Eshun is interested in their interface with technology. He makes an issue of Hancock and the others describing themselves as Afronauts operating outside of the known galaxies and producing 'alien' music. Similarly, in terms of hip-hop, Eshun points out another side of Afrika Bambaataa, in particular, Bambaataa's attempts to 'artificialize himself' through his engagement with industrialised music he borrowed from the European group Kraftwerk. Likewise, Eshun reminds us of Grandmaster Flash's self-description as a 'scientist' working in a research lab (music studio). These post-human perspectives created through the African diasporan interface with technology are called by Eshun *Black Atlantic Futurism*.[26]

For African-Caribbean theologians, the idea of Black people trying to 'artificialise' or transcend human forms through technology is *new*. However, the idea of physical transportation to other worlds or planets is not unheard of in Black Atlantic theologies. Eshun's Afrodelic space programme has an equivalent in Black Atlantic other-worldly theologies. In twentieth-century African-Caribbean history there are narratives of Black people escaping this world by focusing on other planets and worlds. The example par excellence is Alexander Bedward's movement in Jamaica in the early part of the twentieth century. Bedward and his followers believed that they would fly away to heaven on a given date. Like Afrofuturism, Bedwardites saw themselves as aliens: children of God marooned on planet Earth. In the case of Bedward it was biblical prophecy rather than technology that provided the interface and *transformative devices* to travel from this world to the next.

From my reading of Eshun, Black Atlantic Futurism (BAF) in music has several characteristics. Two central ideas have

theological significance for reviewing my redemptive con-
clusions about hip-hop and rap. However, while I must take
on board Eshun's criticism, I also want to show that his anti-
redemption is not as 'anti' as he suggests.

Context does not matter

First, Eshun argues that BAF is not concerned with context.
For hip-hop, this means that the 'street' is no longer the place
where Black music reality is legitimated. Instead, the turntable,
computer and music machines converge to form a laboratory
where new sounds or 'sonic fictions' are created. Hence, Eshun
is concerned with 'computer' music, not 'Black social realities'.
The latter do not exist in the keyboard, sampler and other rhythm
machines.[27]

According to Eshun, within this genre the future is being
created, the past with its genealogies of Black music traditions
is dispensed with, functioning only as a resource to be mined or
'motion captured' for grooves. In other words, in his turntable
theory, tradition and chronology are dispensed with and replaced
by intervals, breaks and gaps drawn from wherever and whatever.[28] In contrast to my analysis of turntable science, in Eshun's
turntable theory, sound is released and separated from any
social responsibility.[29] In opposition to my redemptive and resistance analyses of the mix and the break, here science and
technology are bound on the quest for the *unknown*, not a
communal consciousness concerned with challenging social
oppression.[30] However, not all Black science fiction analysts
share the belief that the quest for the unknown is devoid of social
responsibility.

For example, Black science fiction writer Samuel Delaney
argues that through his futuristic writing he attempts to ask
questions and raises issues pertinent to today's disenfranchised
peoples. In this case, science fiction can be analysed for codes,
symbols and figures that challenge ideas and situations today.

Analysing Eshun's ideas of sonic fiction from this perspective would require an addressing of the contextual forces that fuel Black people's attempts to artificialise themselves as aliens through technologised music in the White-dominated Western world. Such socio-political explanations for Black people's engagement with post-soul Black Atlantic Futurism exist. Take, for example, Paul Gilroy's analysis of the Afrodelic space narratives in the 1970s. Commenting on George Clinton's mid-1970s album cover, depicting Clinton as an astronaut in a space ship in an urban ghetto, Gilroy asks:

> Is he arriving or departing? I have argued before that images like this express a utopian desire to escape from the order of racial oppression, as well as a cosmic pessimism that despairs over the possibility of actual flight.[31]

What is beneficial from Eshun's disposal of contextual analysis is that Black Atlantic Futurism provides a 'space' where the significance of 'race' is dissolved. In other words, his turntable science proposes an anti-essentialist dream where an individual is assessed on the basis of the 'content of character rather than skin colour'. Even so, Eshun's avoidance of socio-political context is problematic from the standpoint of redemptive vengeance.

Despite the benefits of disposing of context, as far as I am concerned contextual analysis is an important epistemological point of departure. This is because through serious analysis of Black experience we are able to develop relevant questions that resonate with Black existential concerns. Political theologians, such as myself, base this presupposition upon the incarnation – because the Son of God was sent into social locations where ethnicity, history and culture were important, we cannot ignore these factors.

Technological music is alien music

The second characteristic of Black Atlantic Futurism is the disembodiment of the human by technology. Eshun's ideas here become rather complex. Put simply, he argues that technological music found in genres such as hip-hop manufactures a hyper-embodiment. Whereas Du Bois talked of Black people in the West having a double consciousness, Eshun goes a step further by suggesting that Black consciousness is reconfigured through the technology, so that we see ourselves through the electronic eyes of the computer, not the eyes of the White Other (Du Bois).[32] Man + electronics becomes a new rhythm machine cyborg (a bionic human) as the human is changed into an alien: the body becomes a large brain which, 'thinks and feels a sensational mathematics throughout the entire surface of its distributed mind'.[33] As a consequence, the mixing board of Grandmaster Flash *et al.* becomes a science lab, and the studio a spacecraft producing alien music.

Considering Black existence as alien existence has an important logic. The story of slavery becomes a story of alien abduction. Black history is a history of non-human existence. We are not human, because Western societies view us as non- and sub-human. Machine music offers an alternative remedy to the Black humanitarian tradition of seeking inclusion and social justice. Machine music creates an alien world through alien music.

However, by identifying the importance of transcendence, Eshun also contradicts his anti-redemption analysis. This is because creating a fiction, whether sonic or otherwise, where Black folks are placed in charge of their destiny and identity is, on one level, a form of redemption. As religionist Michael Lieb has pointed out, in Black Atlantic cultures the idea of Black technological future is deeply interwoven with ideas of redemption and religion.[34] To sum up, Eshun fails to see such redemptive strands in the music and cosmology created in Black sonic fiction, whereas, in my opinion, creating a cosmology where the brutalities and insecurities of contemporary life are removed can be viewed as an attempt to redeem the present situation. Consider, for example the British machine music band, 4 Hero. One of their tasks is to connect the universe in peace and harmony through the mathematics of music. This quest is inherently redemptive:

> During the time you call One Nine and Eight Nine, in a golden location to the North and West of a vast and ancient city, 4 Hero were gathered together: Four Brothers to the Moon and Stars, the far Striders, Children of the Many Islands. Each individually carried one of the primordial elements, Earth, Air, Fire and Water, which were combined as tools to help in mankind's understanding of the Rhythmic nature of the 3rd planet from the Star it calls Sun.[35]

Viewed from this perspective, machine music becomes another redemptive force in Black Atlantic cultures, revealing a transcendent aesthetic. However, whereas the Black humanitarian project found in the canons of soul music and conscious rap and reggae has outlined a social agenda and political philosophies, the Afrodelic space project, dub and other forms of machine music offers limited political praxis.

In the remainder of this chapter, I want to explore the work of one of rap's most successful female artists, Lauryn Hill. Through a dialogue between her best selling album, *The Miseducation of Lauryn Hill*, and redemptive vengeance, I hope to tease out some of the redemptive themes within her hip-hop album. Moreover, I hope to show that the kind of redemption on offer is limited when compared to my analysis of redemptive vengeance in the origins of hip-hop.

4. The Miseducation of Lauryn Hill

The title of Lauryn Hill's album is appropriated from Carter G. Woodson's classic study, *The Miseducation of the Negro*. However, whereas Woodson's text is concerned with exploring systematic attempts to limit Black socio-political awareness through colonial education within the school system, Hill appropriates 'miseducation' in order to point to hidden or subjugated knowledge learned outside of academic life. Hill's miseducation is concerned with the power of personal experience, self-definition and hope. In sum, her theme is how through teaching and sharing experience Black women and men can begin to survive and thrive. Through the use of biblical imagery, proverb and metaphor, Hill constructs a strong, confrontational but intelligent and sensitive emotional range of songs. The music is also diverse, mixing hip-hop with reggae and soul ballad. Moreover, as producer and writer of the album, Hill not only reveals her musical ability but also, politically speaking, her determination to carve out a space in a male-dominated industry. There are many levels on which we can analyse *The Miseducation of Lauryn Hill*.

First, there are issues of Black feminism that arise throughout the album. In particular, Hill makes implicit, and sometimes explicit, reference to the connections between race, class and gender issues. These themes are most clearly articulated in her advice and admonishing of Black women. Unlike many other political rap artists, Hill resurrects the memory of Black female heroes from African queens (Cleopatra) to African American activists (Betty Shebazz). Hence, on one level, Hill constructs a ghettocentric womanist framework – concerned with articulating and dialoguing with Black women including the 'million women in Philly, Penn'.[36] Hill's Black feminism is concerned with providing a powerful personal/psychological/morale approach. In short, she articulates a personal politics

enshrined in a conservative behaviourism – personal determination and responsibility as a way of 'making it through'. Later,
I will show that there are problems with Hill's analysis of the
situation.

Second, in addition to the womanist framework, there is
also an Afrocentric focus throughout the album. Afrocentric
themes in Hill's album range from exploring common themes
amongst African Americans (history, culture, experience),
linking African Americans to their African past by evoking the
memory of African people and, finally, an implicit critique of
power, gender and aesthetics. While Hill does not embrace the
kind of narrow political agenda and dangerous essentialist
reasoning associated with aspects of Afrocentric thought which
find their way into areas of hip-hop, what I want to suggest is
that Hill's album represents a loose Afrocentrism. By a loose
Afrocentrism, I refer to:

> An emphasis on shared African origins among all Black
> people taking pride in those origins and interest in African
> history and culture – or those aspects of New World
> cultures seen as representing African 'survivals' – and a
> belief that Eurocentric bias has blocked or distorted
> knowledge of Africans and their cultures.[37]

Finally, *The Miseducation of Lauryn Hill* also utilises biblical
and theological themes such as judgement, salvation and
justice – all of which is mixed with the personal conservative
behavioural approach mentioned above. For example in 'Final
Hour', Hill weaves together biblical imagery with African
American history, personal redemption and success, linking
Moses and Aaron with Black resistance in America.

Redemption songs

While there are many levels on which one can analyse this
album, my concern here is with the themes of redemption that

run through it. Within this album there is a particular redemptive schema at work. This is by no means systematically laid out, but can be deduced from a classification of several of the songs within particular thematic clusters. There are three clusters that are of importance to Hill's redemptive scheme. First there is a cluster of songs concerned with *warning* the Black community. These songs explore various 'falls from grace' and are aimed at the 'lost'. Incorporating elements of the 'diss' style within rap music, this first cluster criticises before offering redemption. Second, there is a cluster of songs geared towards *redemption*. These forgiveness songs talk of overcoming through forgiveness, moral transformation or self-love. As will be shown below, these songs draw from aspects of the progressive tradition with rap music. Finally, the third cluster of songs concerns *practice*, that is, how to live a successful life. This third cluster is the smallest grouping.

Warning

Lauryn Hill opens her album with a warning to those she calls the 'Lost Ones'. This song critiques the immorality of an unnamed rap-star. While this person may have benefited from their wrongdoing, this benefit will not continue. Hence the refrain, 'you might win some but you just lost one'. Despite the warnings within the song there are, however, redemptive themes. There are calls for re-evaluation: 'But there come many paths and you must choose one/And of you don't change then the rain soon come.'

Likewise, despite the possibility of impending doom, there is time for repentance: 'Now even when you're gone you can still be reborn/And from the night can arrive the sweet dawn.'

The reason for demanding change arises from a theodicy based on the law of reciprocity – good comes to those who do good and bad to those who do badly to others.

Another warning song is 'Doo Wop (That Thing)'. Here she

'schools' women and men about the superficiality and danger of exploitative relationships. Like a 'warner'[39] in Afro-diasporic religious cultures, she begins by admonishing Black women. Here the critique has three focuses, sexual promiscuity, religious hypocrisy and succumbing to Eurocentric aesthetics. While the first two concerns fit in with the conservative behavioural approach in Hill's canon, the third concern is consistent with the loose Afrocentrism.

For the men the critique is just as venomous. As was the case with the women, there is a critique of lax behaviour amongst Black urban youth. The critique, while penned by Hill, would not be out of place amongst conservative politicians in the US. This is because she attacks and mocks crass materialism, absent fathers, domestic violence and sexual irresponsibility. This form of 'schooling' is not made from some abstract or obscure vantage point. Instead Hill speaks from her experience: 'Now Lauryn is only human, Don't think I haven't been through the same predicament.' Whereas 'Lost Ones' offers redemption, here there is no redemptive plan, only a stern warning: 'you betta watch out.'

The third call-to-repentance song is 'Superstar'. Here the criticism is directed towards the hip-hop community. The central concern is the deterioration of the inspirational and political hip-hop with the sexual-play and materialistic genres.

The result is the failure of hip-hop to offer inspiration: 'music is supposed to inspire, so how come we're not getting no higher.'

In summary, the first cluster of songs are concerned with warning the community, in particular the hip-hop fraternity as well as working-class Black folk. Interestingly, the enemy is not some external force but an internal one, which causes self-deceit, hypocrisy and immorality.

Redemption

The second cluster of songs that are part of a redemptive scheme within *The Miseducation of Lauryn Hill* are concerned with redemption. Redemption occurs on a variety of levels – personal, communal and relational.

Personal

Regarding personal redemption, I turn to the song 'To Zion'. In 'To Zion' Lauryn tells of the trials and deliberations surrounding the birth of her son, 'Zion'. This song is concerned with an ethical choice. As if to set an example to those she warns in 'Doo Wop (That Thing)' and to confirm the practice of her 'reap what you sow' theodicy in 'Lost Ones', Hill tells a personal tale of pro-life decision to keep her unborn child. The central redemptive theme arises out of the decision to ignore the advice of those who wished her to place her career ahead of having a child. She decides to follow her heart and not her head and to proceed with the pregnancy.

There is some very important symbolism at work in this song. Signifying takes place on the biblical concept of 'Zion'. The term 'Zion' is appropriated and reconstituted and given a double meaning: Zion is both hope in God and hope in her son, Zion. As Cheryl Kirk-Duggan has demonstrated, 'signifying' – the renaming and revising of words, concepts and expressions in Black music to provide a double meaning – is a characteristic of African-American music.[40]

Communal

The second form of redemption at work is communal redemption. By communal redemption, I refer to redeeming the African American community. Communal redemption is exhibited in 'Final Hour'. Aspects of this song explore the redressing of the balance of power – 'I'm about to change the focus from the richest to the brokest.' But central to this song is the belief that while material gain and position (money and power) are accessible, what is most important is God's judgement. Therefore it is essential that rappers 'keep their eyes on the final hour'. Here redemption comes from God. According to Hill, God redeems and keeps one's 'deen true'.

Communal rescue is also exhibited in 'Forgive Them Father'. This song is a polemic against deception, exploitation, back-stabbing and the dog-eat-dog cultures both inside and outside of the music industry. Here the rapper makes a distinction between forgiveness and trust. In sum, one can forgive but not re-trust with ease.

Relational

Finally, whereas personal redemption explores personal ethics and communal redemption the saving of the group, relational redemption returns to the well-worn path of male–female relationships. Relational redemption occurs on several tracks, including 'X Factor'. Here Hill tells of a problematic relationship with a man who fails to reciprocate her love.

A similar tale is told in 'When it Hurts So Bad'. However, in 'I Used To Love Him', Hill provides a solution to the problem. Rather than continue to give up her power, she seeks forgiveness from God for the life that she lived and gives thanks for being saved from being 'a foolish man's wife'.

However, these songs of despair and unrequited love must be contrasted with tales of romantic mutuality as expressed in 'Nothing Even Matters'. In contrast, here the relationship is perfect and Hill finds herself lost in the love of a good man. Interestingly in this song, as a woman who has found her perfect love, she adopts particular behaviour, no longer frequenting stores or having manicures.

Practice

The final area concerned with redemption is practice. In response to the trials and tribulation of life, the remedy offered by

Hill is found in holding one's ground and refusing to participate in the system of exploitation. As mentioned above, this approach is a personal moral approach, which is further explored in 'Everything is Everything'. Utilising this Afro-diasporic phrase as a metaphor for causality, Hill encourages and empowers those who stand firm against deception.

The fight is against 'those on top' – the power structures that govern Black lives. Unlike others more clearly in the political rap camp, such as Dead Prez, Hill is not as clear and concise in naming the powers. Hence, rather than encouraging Black folk to 'fight the power', Hill turns to internal conservative values of self-love and hard work in order to unleash the power within.

In recent years the conservative behaviourism has over-taken liberal structural approaches to remedying Black pain.[41] Whereas the former encouraged self-help, discipline, hard work and enterprise, the latter blamed the State and its institutions for the failure of Black progress. However, any meaningful strategy for Black empowerment must be a mixture of these two traditions. Unfortunately in *The Miseducation of Lauryn Hill*, only one side of the equation is adequately explored.

Religious reflection and The Miseducation of Lauryn Hill

So what can be said from a religious-cultural perspective about *The Miseducation of Lauryn Hill*? I want to make three observations before evaluating this album from the perspective of redemptive vengeance.

There are at least two theological motifs which arise in her work. First, the album displays Augustinian hope: anger at the way things are and the courage to change them.[42] But as mentioned above, the focus here is on personal change.

Second, the mixture of Scripture, street politics and urban life represents a form of common-sense theology. Common-sense theology in Afro-diasporic communities is concerned with the ways we have used common wisdom and shared understanding so as to survive and thrive under racist regimes for four hundred years. Common-sense theology is therefore concerned with an articulation and practice of the Christian faith which is grounded in knowledge and experience of 'everyday people' – in this case the interface between hip-hop and Scripture.

Whereas academic theology does theology in order to critique the Church, common-sense theology is a lived theology enabling Black men and women to survive in the workplace, home and streets. Whereas academic theology is found in books, journals and classrooms, common-sense theology's locus is in the hearts, minds and language of Black folk. Common-sense theology is articulated on the tops of buses, street corners, in arcades, homes and sports shops. Finally, whereas academic theology is married to academic traditions, complex ideas, methods and language, common-sense theology is married to street talk, plain speech and clarity. While these traditions are not mutually exclusive, it is a rare theology which incorporates the two.

4. The Miseducation of Lauryn Hill and redemptive vengeance

As mentioned above, redemptive vengeance is concerned with how African-Caribbean people in Britain faced with subtle yet brutal forms of oppression can use their rage in a constructive manner. Aspects of Hill's redemptive schema concur with redemptive vengeance, in particular the need to save ourselves, first and foremost. Hill offers a personal, conservative social and ethical response. This is particularly true in terms of personal redemption. Hill reveals ways in which Black women faced with 'no-good' men can turn their hearts to God and not be consumed with unrighteous anger or self-destruction. Forgiveness also features in *The Miseducation* – indeed, one track is entitled, 'Forgive Them, Father'. As was the case with redemptive vengeance, however, this forgiveness does not relinquish the need for justice in the personal relational sphere. Hence, because Hill's album is more personal than communal, forgiveness occurs in the personal realm. While this is important, it is not complete. This is because many of the problems affecting Black people require a analysis that is concerned with addressing the personal problems that confront us, but also with addressing the social and political structures that oppress us. As with many contemporary African-American rappers there is no critique of capitalism, or political economy, despite Hill wanting Black women to get their slice of the pie, that is, 'get their green too' ('Final Hour'). As Cornel West notes: 'We must begin not with the problem of black people but with the flaws of American society . . . flaws rooted in historic inequalities and longstanding cultural stereotypes.'[43]

In sum, as Paul Gilroy eloquently elaborates in *Against Race*, *The Miseducation of Lauryn Hill* represents a general movement away from the occupation of public-sphere politics.[44] While not being a retreat into the body politics of sexual-play rap, it is a retreat into the personal sphere. Consequently, *The Miseducation of Lauryn Hill*, while a powerful expression of personal empowerment, fails to provide a redemptive vengeance that encourages Black people to take control of the public and social arenas in which our existence is threatened.

In the final chapter, I will demonstrate how redemptive vengeance can move into the public sphere and address structural forces that limit Black life in Britain.

5.
Redeeming the hustler (Part 1): Black male offenders and redemptive vengeance

Introduction

In Chapter 3, I explored a personal way that redemptive vengeance challenged me to rethink the Beckford name and identity. In Chapter 4, I examined an aspect of Black popular culture in reaction to redemptive vengeance. In this concluding chapter, I want to discover what it means to view redemptive vengeance as a socio-political tool challenging both individuals and structures in contemporary Britain. Redemptive vengeance is not only bothered with individual and private matters but also propels me into the social world to ask questions and find solutions to the problems that confront urban African-Caribbean people. There are a plethora of issues that one might address. Family, community apathy, political disenfranchisement and education are but a few. Redemptive vengeance, however, is concerned with how Black people can redeem these situations.

In my case one area in which I have a major concern is with Black incarceration – the high rate of incarceration of Black men and women. In cities such as Birmingham, there is often a larger percentage of African-Caribbean men and women in prison than in higher education. While the issues of Black female incarceration are also important, in this first exploration of crime and theology, I will focus on Black males. This is because, at the time of writing this chapter, my exposure and dialogue was in the context of Black men. I hope that my dialogue with Black women in prison will appear in written form in future publications.

I became involved in prison work as a result of my thinking on redemptive vengeance. In sum, one way of channelling my concerns over the plight of Black males within the prison system was to infiltrate the system and engage in dialogue with Black men to explore ways in which we can understand and even redeem aspects of the social, political and moral realities that lie behind Black male incarceration. My desire was to offer some of the thinking involved in redemptive vengeance as a resource for Black offenders. In order to have any meaningful dialogue with offenders it was necessary for me to admit my own biases, namely, despite being born and raised and still living in a working-class African-Caribbean inner-city region of Birmingham, my social class and professional location together gave me more opportunity for analytical reflection than many of the working-class men I was to engage with. The worst outcome would be to present myself as a 'Black professional saviour' with the 'cure' for working-class Black men. The best that I could hope to become was an 'organic intellectual' (see p. 50) engaged in critical solidarity with my 'brothers' inside. In racist and classist societies, poorer Black men will get caught up in the criminal justice system. Let me explain.

Go to jail: do not pass Go

In White supremacist, capitalist, patriarchal societies, where the same establishment controls wealth creation, the schools and the prisons, a large percentage of working-class Black, African-Caribbean people will get caught up in the criminal justice system. Unfortunately under the 'New Labour' government of Tony Blair there is an unwillingness to develop meaningful strategies that transform discriminatory practices within education and the criminal justice system. In order to find meaningful strategies it is necessary to make clear the structural forces which ensnare Black men. To this end, I draw from two schools of thought: *left realism* and *critical race theory*.

Left realism

This approach to the analysis of crime identifies the ways in which the structural position of Black people and racist policing contributes to the criminalisation of Black people. The logic behind this argument is that relative deprivation caused by discrimination, disadvantage and economic marginalisation leads to crime. In short, marginalised youth from deprived neighbourhoods commit crime. Left realists such as Lea and Young[1] apply theories of lower-class youth crime to crime among Black youth, with 'race' providing an additional variable. In short, racism within policing and the criminal justice system results in Black deviancy being exaggerated or stereotyped on racist lines. While theorists differ on the methods and analytical focuses for analysing data and attitudes, what is clear is that Black people who enter the criminal justice system cannot expect to be treated fairly before the law. Black African Caribbeans are more likely to be arrested and more likely to be prosecuted than cautioned when compared with their White peers. We also are more likely to be given custodial sentences rather than community service sentences, compared with our White counterparts.[2]

Critical race theory

Whereas left realism focuses on structural forces, critical race theory makes race its central concern. Critical race theory shows how in capitalist societies such as Britain with a long history of slave and colonial exploitation of Black people, it has been difficult to erase racialised oppression from structural processes such as the criminal justice system. Critical race theory encourages us to take a broader look at crime and its role within processes of racism. The logic that is at work here is that although white-collar crimes such as fraud, embezzlement and tax evasion are a more expensive loss to the national purse than so called 'working-class crimes' such as property theft and street crime, it has been convenient for right- and left-wing governments to focus on street crime and Black youth in order to scapegoat Black people as one of the causes of crime.

The racialisation of crime is most clearly demonstrated in police and media myths about Black crime as a problem. Take for example the statement of the former Metropolitan Police chief, Sir Paul Condon, in 1995 that 80 per cent of those robbed in London identified young Black males as responsible. Interestingly, what Sir Paul did not say was why the police were prioritising this kind of crime when there were many other offences that could be targeted apart from street crime. In addition, the racial dimension is misleading because young males dominate offences in street crime across the UK. Therefore, in Glasgow it would be young white males, and similarly in the Home Counties the offenders would be mostly White. In contrast, in inner-city London with a large pool of Black males, Black males dominate the crime statistics. Hence the racialisation of street crime: suggesting that Black men are more likely to commit crime is not an accurate piece of criminal data but a symptom of the ways in which crime facts are often more political than legal.

Response by the Black Church

For fifty years Black Churches have been partially alert to this situation, and have involved themselves at various levels of the criminal justice system to address some of the social and political factors that cause Black crime. There are two traditions of action.

The *indirect* approach has viewed the Black Church as a place of rescue and shelter for Black pilgrims in a strange land. The role of the Church, as well as offering personal salvation, is to protect, support and offer guidance to Black men. Therefore, just by virtue of its existence, the Church offers an alternative culture to the culture of crime. For example, during the Brixton uprising of 1981, Black Church leaders commended themselves on the fact that their Church members were not involved in the class-based multicultural resistance to racist policing, because the Church had taught its members to respect property and the law.

The *direct* approach is concerned with actively engaging with the criminal justice system in order to bring about change. There are two forms of activity. First, a multitude of Black majority churches have rightly taken an evangelistic approach and viewed African-Caribbean people in prison as a mission field. In this case, prisoners are 'souls' to be saved. These churches sends choirs, evangelists and preachers to prison chapels on Sunday mornings to preach the good news to those in prison. For example, my local church, Trinity Fellowship in Handsworth, has been involved in prison ministry at Brinsford Young Offenders Institute for several years. The strength of this approach is that it challenges prisoners to think about their lives from a Black spiritual perspective. The weakness is that it fails to explore the complex social and political forces that contribute to Black crime. Second, a few churches have become involved in the welfare of prisoners and their families. For example, in Birmingham, the African Caribbean Evangelical Alliance runs 'Prison Link', an organisation dedicated to social welfare amongst the families of Black prisoners. The main area of participation in prison welfare involves financial, social and spiritual support for offenders and their families. While these approaches have been extremely beneficial to the well-being of the prisoners' families, they are limited in their role of addressing the wider social causes of crime and the personal motivation of the offender.

Redemptive vengeance and Black offenders

These church responses are on the whole commendable. However, what is culpable is the inability of the Black Church to find a response that tackles both the structural causes of crime and the personal motivation of the offender – in other words a response that combines the personal behaviouralism mentioned in the work of Lauryn Hill with the structural themes in left realism and critical race theory. Hence, in order to apply redemptive vengeance to the arena of Black male incarceration it was necessary to develop a response that would focus on structures and motivations. This is the focus of this chapter, with the aim of moving towards a redemptive vengeance for Black offenders.

There are three parts to this study. I begin with the theological presuppositions that underpin my approach. After this, I will show how these presuppositions assist with a methodological framework for working with Black offenders. I will end by exploring some of the outcomes of this dialogue – in particular, how reflection on film enabled the men to assess their lives and also the values that they hold. Finally, I will contour a redemptive vengeance for Black offenders and prison ministry in the UK.

Theological presuppositions

There are four motifs that govern this pursuit of critical solidarity. These are Black theology, prison as a mission field, the jubilee and reparation.

Black liberation theology is for 'the least of these'

Black theology makes its existential starting point the themes, concerns and aspirations of the Black community.

Through a dialogue between Scripture, Church and Black cultures, Black theology seeks to locate and augment the liberating message of Jesus to the oppressed both inside and outside of the Black community.

Black theology takes seriously the call of God to be concerned with the 'least of these' in our society. Matthew 25 suggests that one category within the 'least of these' are offenders – 'I was in prison and you visited me'. As mentioned above, Black African-Caribbean men are more likely to be stopped by the police, will get a longer sentence than their White counterparts if convicted, and face victimisation, racism and oppression within the prison system. In response to Matthew 25, African-Caribbean offenders constitute an important focus for Black theological attention.

Prison is a mission field

Because of the controlling nature of incarceration in Black communities (critical race theory) one approach to redeeming this oppressive situation is to make prison a positive transformative process for Black men, a kind of morale renewal and leadership training. This is not a new idea in Black Atlantic cultures, as many Black religious and social organisations have viewed Black offenders as a primary mission field. Example par excellence is the Nation of Islam in the UK and USA. Moreover, while the Black Church in Britain has also taken this view (prison as a mission field) it has not explored the historic role prison has played in producing Black leaders. For example, both Malcolm X and Dr King spent significant and formative time in prison. So here, mission is more than just 'saving souls' – it offers an alterative view of Black incarceration in general and Black male incarceration in particular.

Jubilee: set the captives free

Third, in St Luke 4:18–19, Jesus' proclamation of his mission, we are told that release for prisoners is one of his tasks. Drawing on the Jubilee language of Isaiah 61, Jesus equates his mission with that of social justice and social equalisation traditions in Israel. In Black theological thought Jesus' proclamation is the basis for the liberation of oppressed peoples. The African-American Black liberation theologian James Cone argues that divine revelation expresses solidarity between the mission of Jesus and the oppressed:

> The theme of God's liberation of the poor continued in the story of Jesus' reading in the Nazareth synagogue from the book of Isaiah . . . After the reading, Jesus commented, 'Today in your very hearing this text has come true', thus tying the promise of deliverance to his own mission.[3]

Not all Black theologians, however, concur on the liberative import of the life and death of Jesus. In contrast to Cone, the womanist theologian Delores Williams argues that an image of Jesus as the one who enables *survival* (rather than liberation) is more consistent with the promise of Jesus amongst marginalised people. For Williams, a legitimate response to the situation is to articulate a theology of empowerment for people whose existence is under threat.[4] I do not see Cone and Williams at odds here. Instead, their two approaches lie at opposite poles of a survival–liberation spectrum where liberation emerges out of the survival of oppressed people. In regard to African-Caribbean men in British prisons, Jesus' message is of great significance. Setting the prisoners free becomes a motif for, at best, liberation and, at least, survival.

Reparation: I will repay

As mentioned in Chapter 2, redemptive vengeance calls for restitution. I suggest that an important paradigm of restitution is demonstrated in the Letter to Philemon where Paul offers to 'repay' Philemon compensation for the losses he has suffered due to Onesimus' absence. The theme and action of restitution for Black men in the criminal justice system is an important dimension of redemption. Restitution is an external and also internal. It focuses on 'doing time' in prison as 'payment for crime' and also on the substantive 'heart' change that is an internal commitment to new ways of being. Reparation is also important because it brings the victim back into the crime equation. That is to say, reparation shows the offender that there must be atonement for their crime not only to the State that has imprisoned them but also to the victims that they have damaged.

I will now outline the method that emerges from my theological presumptions.

Methodology

This method was worked out over a period of six months with a group of African-Caribbean prisoners in Birmingham prison. There are three distinct phases in our methodology. I was influenced by the counter-hegemonic epistemologies at work in Black feminist and Third World theorists as well as the hermeneutical paradigms that emerge from Black and other liberation theologians. Drawing on these influences there are three related ideas at work here: experience, dialogue and action.

Experience

All theology emerges from a social location and is therefore biased in some way. For example, I make my starting point Black urban experience in Britain. Black experience, however, is not singular but hybrid and diverse. Therefore, it is always important to recognise that by making Black experience my starting point, I do so in a specific way related to my theological outlook, class positioning and ethnicity.

Likewise, the Black offenders make their life experiences the starting point, in particular, issues of race, class and gender arising in and through incarceration. It was not possible to address every single aspect of Black prison life in these sessions, but what was important to me was the use of redemption as an organising principle. What I am concerned with here is, how can Black men turn their lives around in prison? A useful trope for all of us was the notion of the 'hustler' and the 'hustle' culture amongst the offenders. The 'hustler' is a complex characterisation. As James Messerschmidt shows, the hustler is an oppositional character noted for 'refusing to allow legitimate work to become the primary signifier of identity, privileging of leisure, and emphasizing "fast money" involving little or non-physical labour'.[5] While the hustler is a oppositional masculinity he is not always concerned with hegemonic capitalist control. Later I will show that there were two hustler mentalities at work in the experience of the prisoners. These are the *maintenance* and the *misfortunate* logics of crime.

Dialogue

A second component within my method is dialogue. As Patricia Hill Collins states, dialogue enables sharing between two equal subjects.[6] Dialogue is important in this context because I did not want to go into the classroom as an expert or wisdom-teacher but instead, as a brother, amongst brothers – all of us with valid perspectives and opinions.

This kind of dialogue is not new in the African-Caribbean context. Arguably the most important and relevant for me is that which occurred between the Black intellectual Walter Rodney and proletarian revolutionary Rastas in Jamaica in the early 1970s. Rodney brought a critical and intellectual focus to the Rastafarian movement, in particular, tools for a historical and material analysis of the Jamaican situation. In return the proletarian Rastas provided Rodney with cultural resources for an alternative and counter-hegemonic intellectualism. What I am suggesting here is that the academy can learn from Black offenders and vice versa. The final methodological concern is 'texts'.

Common text: film

It was important to find common texts with which both the offenders and I felt comfortable, and which were fair to everyone. I learned quickly that written material did not suit everyone, because of the varying degrees of literacy within the group. Hence, literacy became an issue of exclusion, as some men were more able to participate than others. In contrast, whenever I used film to illustrate various points or themes, this proved a more successful resource – that is, there was wider participation in the discussion. Hence, by consensus, film became the primary text through which we would explore ideas and concepts related to redemption. The use of film reaffirmed my belief that in a post-literate age the visual image is where the great ideological battles are fought over meaning, identity and politics. By using film, we were not only exploring religious and cultural motifs but also, as Black men, we were learning to critique and deconstruct, engaging in the politics of representation and other semiotic concerns. However, it was necessary to develop a framework for analysing film. To this end, I returned to my thinking elsewhere on the interface between Black religion and Black culture.

Religious cultural criticism

Elsewhere, I have articulated the need for diasporan African people to utilise the interface between Black religion and Black culture in the search for a political theology. While religious cultural criticism encourages and facilitates dialogue amongst Black religious communities in Britain, I have chosen to develop a Black *theological* approach, which is concerned with asking Black theological questions about Black expressive cultures. This form of Black theological cultural criticism is informed by Theophus Smith's analysis of Black expressive culture in the African-American context, where he describes Black expressive cultures as having the ability to heal and also do harm. To express these concerns Smith describes Black cultures as *pharmacopoeic*.[7] The pharmacopoeic nature of culture encourages us to ask theological and ethical questions about Black expressive cultures both inside and outside of the Black Church. This is because not all of Black culture is sustaining or uplifting. Such an analysis of culture must also acknowledge the relationships between expressive cultures and other social forces such as power, domination and resistance. One purpose of this analysis is to identify those aspects of Black expressive cultures that enable the sustenance, encouragement and liberation of Black people in Britain. As Black culture is a resource for Black theology, locating healing streams in Black culture enables meaningful dialogue between the theology and culture. In this case the cultural site of analysis is film.

Film: identity and textual themes

The task here is to make the experience of the men the context for a religious-cultural reflection on themes within the film. Regarding the latter, we worked with two guiding focuses. These were *identity themes* and *textual themes*.

Identity themes explore character and characterisation. On the one hand, they explore stereotyping, in particular the ways in which Black people are reduced to fixed moral roles related to a perceived inherent essence. As Eugene Franklin Wong's[8] materialist analysis of stereotyping in Hollywood film has demonstrated, the net result of stereotyping is that 'a group's stereotyped image tends to oscillate between two simple poles: good and bad, noble and savage, loyal and traitorous, kind-hearted and villainous.'[9] While an analysis of stereotypes can be limited, it served a useful purpose here, in particular by its ability to identify that which is by consensus deemed progressive, or to eliminate racisms.

Textual themes concern aesthetics, language and formal features of production. Here, through analysis of symbols, codes, camera angles and positioning, the viewer can evaluate issues of economics, power, difference and politics. As a result, it is possible to look beyond so-called 'positive characters' into a world of aesthetics and semiotics, which suggest an alternative 'textual oppression' at work. A useful example of this process in action is the hugely successful Hugh Grant and Julia Roberts' film *Notting Hill*. Here a world is created where Black people are absent from view or located in the distance of wide-angle long shots. All of which points to a relationship between film production and racial ideology.[10]

The net result of this process was that offenders were able to make critical connections between the movie 'reel' and the personal 'reality' of their lives. For example, after watching *Mo' Better Blues* one offender related the life of the main character Bleek and his treatment of women to his own life:

The most important film we watched so far is *Mo' better Blues*. The character who I feel I can relate to is Bleek who is play by Denzel Washington. By watching that film I could see myself in the film i.e. the way Bleek treated his two main girls who he think (*sic*) that everything has to be run the way he wanted to.

Examples of how textual matters arise are found in the films *Malcolm X* and *When We Were Kings*. Regarding the former, an offender asked why Spike Lee (the director) had given such prominence to his character 'Shorty'. This observation enabled the group to explore the codes and symbols at work within the narrative and cinematography of the film, through watching Spike Lee as a successful African-American male. The views within the group ranged from seeing Spike as a middle-class Black Nationalist attempting to equate his personal struggle and ambition with the life of Malcolm X, to viewing Spike's role as a glorified stylistic twist in the manner perfected by Alfred Hitchcock. Another example emerged from the film, *When We Were Kings*. One offender states: 'Black women in the film were very much in the background and like they were there to serve their husbands.' In this case the student made critical observations about the role of women within the drama of Ali's fight with Frazier in the mid 1970s.

Action

I did not want the work that we were doing to stay in the classroom, even though it was a prison classroom filled with intelligent working-class Black men. Therefore, I tried always to link our thinking with the life experiences of the men before, during and possibly after prison. Because of the limited confines of the prison, action was restricted to challenging attitudes and values and hopefully impacting behaviour now and in the future. This raised a significant issue. While much of my analysis, writing and life have been concerned with structural analysis that is exploring the complex interplay between race, class and gender in Black oppression, in the context of prison this analysis was more dangerous than in the university context. Mobilising

Black offenders in a prison classroom is perceived as a threat to the prison authorities. On several occasions I was discouraged and warned by prison officers against trying to change the men I was working with. Action was also about how the dialogue changed me as a professional theologian and as a Black man, which I will discuss at a later date.

Maintenance and misfortune

There were a variety of themes which I explored with offenders. The classes were structured as all-day seminars in the prison education department at Birmingham prison. The morning was spent watching the film and the afternoon with analysis. The analysis consisted of questions that the men wanted to raise, and also issues that had arisen while watching the film. Readers from Caribbean or Caribbean diasporan households such as mine will know that watching film is often a form of call and response! We talk out our expressions, concerns and ideas as we watch what is going on. As a result there is a continual volley of comments, statements and thoughts from the audience. The discussion also consisted of themes the men had raised verbally while watching the film as well as the themes they omitted. That is to say, what was not said was as important as what was mentioned.

During the course of the year, I explored three major groups of topics with the men. There were a group of films concerned with understanding crime. These films were geared towards understanding their interpretation of race, class and gender issues. A flagship film in this category was *Set it Off* (1996). In this film three Black women, for various social and moral reasons, make a decision to engage in crime – bank robberies. What was important here was to examine the motivations of the three women in order to develop models of criminal incentive. After this, the offenders discussed and discerned which motives were just and which were unjust. It was significant that only 'Stony' (Jada Pinkett) was considered to have a legitimate reason for her involvement in crime because her motives were not driven by greed but personal 'revenge' (the police had unjustly killed her brother as a result of mistaken identity). In contrast, the issues of racism, sexism and poverty that affected the other central characters (Frankie and Tisean) were considered less important motivations.

Another cluster of films were those explicitly concerned with redemption, in particular, the experiences of men who had turned their lives around in prison contexts. For example, a defining film was *American History X* (1998), the story of the conversion of a Neo-Nazi. What was particularly significant about this film is that 'Derek' (Edward Norton) is redeemed by two Black males: one inside prison and one outside. Furthermore, as an act of atonement Derek is required not only to change as a person but also to 'clean up' the mess he created as a former leader of a Nazi group. As was the case with Zacchaeus (Luke 19:1–10), his conversion experience required restitution. The purpose of this second cluster of films was to explore the process of redemption on film and compare and contrast how these models worked for the men.

Finally, the third group were concerned with gender politics. Regarding gender politics, a central film was *Mo' Better Blues* (1990). This is a Spike Lee film about a self-absorbed jazz musician, Bleek Gilliam (Denzel Washington). Bleek's obsession with music is contrasted with his treatment of his 'women'. Not only does he have several women 'on the go', but also his treatment of them is casual and only sexual. By using Bleek as a model of Black male sexism, this and similar films enabled the men to create a space for discussing issues surrounding the treatment of Black women by Black men, and also in society.

So what can be learned from this dialogue with Black male prisoners? There are two areas in which I would like to explore these questions: the offenders' self-understanding of crime and of redeeming the hustler mentality. Regarding the first point, there were two positions that the offenders articulated. These were the *maintenance* and the *misfortune logic of crime*. While I present these views as separate, they were in reality much more interrelated in the thinking of the offenders. This is because their self-understanding would change regarding specific offences as well as changing over a period of time or depending on circumstances.

Maintenance logic of crime

I want to call the first position the maintenance logic of crime. This position consists of three related ideas. First, we live in an unequal society. Therefore some people by virtue of class and race will be outsiders and have less access to resources and opportunities. Second, equalisation cannot occur through the natural channels because the systems and processes are organised to favour those already with power and status. Third, as a result, specific types of crimes geared towards giving the outsiders a chance to better themselves in the long term are justified. In this sense certain types of crime are legitimate responses to systemic marginalisation.

As one offender wrote:

Poverty paralyses and crushes one's spirit. If we are self reliant [i.e. through crime] yet it enables us to be partially out of trials and tribulations . . . the basic needs of people must be catered for.

The maintenance logic, I later discovered, is not dissimilar to the traditional Marxist argument that in capitalist societies, those denied legitimate access to wealth creation will turn to crime. However, whereas Marxists view crime as a sort of political resistance, among the prisoners the motivation was to improve their standard of living, or to maintain a particular standard of living. For example, in one conversation a prisoner argued that he needed to commit crime in order to make sure that he could live in a decent area and drive a good car.

The maintenance logic of crime has great appeal. This is because it takes seriously the racialised inequalities that are deeply embedded in British society. For the conscious offenders with an eye on Black history, the maintenance logic was seen as being loosely related to the Black Atlantic intellectual tradition articulated by Marcus Garvey in the Caribbean, and by W. E. B Du Bois towards the end of his life. Both believed that while African people remained in the West, the majority would be forced to live their lives as outsiders, never managing to be accepted to the heart or centre of white society.

From the perspective of redemptive vengeance the maintenance logic is problematic for several reasons. Much of the crime committed by the Birmingham offenders was against other Black people, so that it was the Black community that suffered disproportionately from this 'outsider' mentality. This rationale, therefore, could not be considered a form of Black resistance or as having any meaningful political quality, as suggested in old left theories of structured crime. Also, the maintenance logic had no redeeming qualities, as it was based on a selfish world-view. For example, prison, within this viewpoint, was a place for new criminal education. One notorious drugs baron stated:

> Yes, I would say prison have rearrange me (*sic*) in a way, been to prison over the past few months I have learn crime more than anything else.

From my standpoint, I was keen to show the offenders that the 'maintenance logic' colludes with the attempts of postcolonial Britain to subjugate and sedate Black people. Black men are deluded into thinking that there are no other ways in which we can beat oppression. From the standpoint of the offenders, some of the men within the group were willing to accommodate the maintenance logic if it could be seen as allowing them to make good in the long run. However, there were others who viewed the maintenance logic as a selfish outlook because, within the prison, maintenance-logic offenders were the least benevolent and least altruistic group. As one offender said in a discussion, 'I don't know any drugs man who has built a school in the community.'

Misfortune logic

The second position I want to call the misfortune logic. Whereas the maintenance logic favoured the career criminal, non-career criminals generally held the misfortune logic. This group recognised that we live in an unequal society and that some people by virtue of class and race will be outsiders and have less access to resources and opportunities. They believed, however, that equalisation could occur through non-criminal activity – by virtue of ingenuity or hard work. Their understanding of their incarceration was that it resulted from failed opportunism: they had taken a chance or risk involving crime and had been caught. The misfortune camp was more likely to see prison as a means of reform and deterrent than was the maintenance camp.

There was a positive resonance between redemptive vengeance and the misfortune position. Men who held to this view were generally more willing to explore the wider social issues that led to their incarceration as well as their personal motivations. Moreover, this group were more willing to explore ways in which prison could be a redemptive experience within their lives. For example, one prisoner, responding to the redemptive themes within the film *American History X*, wrote:

> Redemption is the passing from one (inferior) state, ie sin
> enslavement or imprisonment into another better or
> higher state ie grace, freedom. In that sense prison itself
> could not be seen as redemption but to the Individual can

be seen as part of the process of redemption . . . Giving a person time for reflection.

Furthermore, misfortune logic adherents were more likely to explore ways in which redemption beyond themselves might be actualised outside of prison. As one offender wrote of himself:

> One could blame society, unemployment or drugs for my constant re-offending. Deep within myself, I know there's a number of reasons or excuses. I am now very lucky to go to education classes. I am at present undergoing a training course. I hope to gain a qualification as a basic literary tutor. It's something positive to come out of a negative situation. What I do with it when I get out I have yet to decide. I will definitely look to do something practical so as to prevent others falling foul to the same vicious circle where there's not very many people who give a shit about other people.

The maintenance and misfortune perspectives were played out in various themes that arose in the films or discussions. In order to elaborate on the two perspectives I want to briefly touch on three themes. These are, *violence, consumerism* and *punishment.*

Violence

While the misfortune camp generally disagree with the use of unprovoked violence and would affirm violence only as a form of self-defence, in contrast, the majority of the maintenance camp argue that violence is a legitimate method of problem-solving. There are two parts to this argument. We live in a violent world where notions of non-violence are used to prevent the weak from obtaining resources and status. In other words, the powerful act with violent laws etc. but expect the marginal-ised to act with non-violence. In such cases, not to utilise violence, particularly when defending oneself, is to accept patterns of oppression and restriction. The real question is not about violence vs. non-violence, but what level of violence is necessary to ensure that one has sufficient resources to live and prosper.

From the perspective of redemptive vengeance, as I have argued in Chapter 2, the danger with this kind of thinking is that the violence tends to be fratricidal and out of control. As a consequence, the spiral of violence continues unchecked. My concern was to explore ways in which in White supremacist, capitalist, patriarchal societies Black male violence was used to control and limit. Therefore, while accepting the men's presuppositions about the 'unreal' nature of non-violence, it was important to offer them alternative ways to avoid violence. As is the case with the analysis of material goods and punishment, the outcome of dialogue on this theme is ongoing.

Material goods

In general there was very little difference in opinion between the maintenance and misfortune camps regarding the acquisition of goods and conspicuous consumption as a valid pursuit. However, differences existed on how these goods might be obtained. While the misfortune camp were more willing to reject violence, the maintenance camp argued that it is justifiable to utilise the logic of crime or violence as part of this endeavour. In other words the logic of crime and violence are the lesser good, which make possible the acquisition and consumption of material goods. Placed within the wider context of a capitalist society, this suggests that these men as a subgroup have internalised the capitalist dream of prosperity through hard work, but have chosen to differ as regards the means of achieving this end. This reaffirmed my belief that resistance and political protest were not a part of the criminological framework of the majority of the men I was working with.

The belief in 'material good' was linked to the perceived

failings of the African-Caribbean first generation who, it was often argued, had not achieved as much as they should have. For example, giving his reasons for valuing material goods, one prisoner from Handsworth continually argued that his father had 'done everything by the book all of his life in England but lived in poverty in Handsworth'. He did not want to end up like his father. However, having spent half of his adult life in prison with very little to show for it, he was inadvertently on course to achieve less than his father. My response to this value was twofold: first, to offer alternative ideas on the meaning of 'wealth', that is, well-being is more than material and financial; second, to offer non-market values such as the value of conservation and to point out the moral, spiritual and social dangers of consumption to both continental and diasporan Africans.

Plausibility of punishment

Finally, the last theme that arose as a focus for religious-cultural reflection on film was the role of prison. As mentioned above, for those in the misfortune camp, prison was a tragic event, the end-product of actions and circumstances that they do not condone. In contrast, for the maintenance group, prison was a part of the process of crime. In short, the logic of crime involves a high level of risk. In response to this risk, many of the men realised that breaking the law would lead to legal sanctions. Therefore prison and punishment was, for some, an integral dimension of striving for the acquisition of more material goods. Hence the colloquial saying, 'prison is an occupational hazard'.

My contribution to this guiding theme was a 'reality check'. I pointed out that the problem here was that, for the vast majority, the time in prison outweighed the gains from crime. That is to say, more of them spend time in prison, on the run or living in fear, than living the 'ideal' type of criminal life: 'living large'. Therefore, punishment was more realistic an option than many of the men would like to admit. Because of what I presumed to be a state of denial expressed in the belief that 'I will not get caught next time', my concern was to (1) demythologise the repeat-offending reality for Black offenders within the framework of analysis, (2) introduce the idea of redemptive vengeance – that is, to find creative and meaningful ways of redeeming and thereby transforming their lives.

Redeeming the hustler

So what can be concluded from the early stages of this dialogue between redemptive vengeance and Black offenders? There are three issues that will guide my contribution; they may also be of use to those embracing redemptive vengeance.

First, redemptive vengeance cannot just be the concern of Black middle-class people facing the glass ceiling in Britain's professional playing fields. It must become a resource for all of the Black community. Of particular importance are the outsiders within our community, including those who are incarcerated. Second, redemptive vengeance demands a dialogue between Black professionals and the prison. In particular, Black academics must find creative spaces for subverting the forces that victimise and criminalise Black people. Third, this dialogue must make mutual redemption its core. Black prisoners have insights and viewpoints that we must engage with if we are to offer any meaningful strategy for their survival and even emancipation. Conversely, professional Black people can offer solidarity and solutions. Solidarity is concerned with recognising the mutuality of our struggle. We can also offer insights and perspectives alongside those offered by offenders. Fourth, redemptive vengeance necessitates a structural and personal analysis of crime. That is to say, as well as exploring social forces it must also take seriously psychological forces. Finally, redemptive vengeance means that we have to find common resources that inform our struggle. In this case film has provided the resource for analysis, and hopefully it will also provide the basis for a new articulation of redemptive vengeance that attempts in one way to engage with the prisons in Europe, North America and the Caribbean that are spilling over with Black people.

Conclusion

It has been my intention in this book to provide hope, empowerment and resources for those concerned with fighting racism in Britain with a theological paradigm capable of addressing the difficult times in which we live, minister and serve God. In particular, I have explored briefly several ways in which Black rage, engendered by personal attack and through the politics of representation, might be redeemed by African-Caribbean people in Britain.

On a personal level, writing this book has been of great significance. I have realised that I have spent a lot of wasted time in the past, fuming over the treatment of Black people and getting enraged about how those with power use representation to continue the oppression of Black men and women. I did not have a meaningful theological framework that enabled me to use my rage in such a way that it addressed the issues so as to allow me bring my faith as a Christian into the arena of Black struggle in a way that would be sustaining, enabling and empowering. However, conceptualising an approach to these concerns in the form of redemptive vengeance has made considerable difference in my own life.

Having contemplated the subject of Black rage through writing this book, I now find that my conversation with students, colleagues and friends on the subject of Black rage has changed. Rather than feeling depressed, enraged, damaged or immobilised by the rage caused by problematic inclusion and pernicious exclusion, I now view my rage as a productive emotion, which has power to save and transform. That is, my rage is a catalyst for personal and social change consistent with the call of God to be full of the Spirit and also battle against the principalities and powers of this world that seek to demean and destroy through oppressive practices, systems and institutions.

I am not suggesting that redemptive vengeance is an easy theological idea to live out, especially when we consider some of the brutal and distressing factors facing Black people. For example, at the moment of writing, my Saturday newspapers (25 March 2000) are full of interviews and analysis of the alleged racially motivated stabbing of the White boyfriend of a Black British athletics star, Asia Hansen. Racial terror continues to be a feature of British life. As I have stated within the covers of this book, forgiveness and creating a space for new beginnings are a gift from God.

Because forgiveness is God's gift, redemptive vengeance, guided by the power of the Kingdom of God to challenge the principalities and powers of this world, offers a powerful antidote. By focusing on saving ourselves and developing an environment for change and seeking out ways in which we can actively transform the situation, redemptive vengeance promotes justice and encourages Black people not to give up on our quest for reparation in the past or present. As a consequence redemptive vengeance is an important rebuff to the forces of racialised oppression. Redemptive vengeance, while being primarily concerned with the personal sphere of Black life, is not individual but communal and social, that is, it is concerned with empowering Black men and women to seek out and destroy the forces of oppression, whether motivated by racism, sexism or classism. This is why, in Chapter 5, I explored how redemptive vengeance could provide the motivating force behind dialogue between the academy and the prison. In short, I propose redemptive vengeance as a powerful tool for prophetic ministry, as it is multi-dimensional, concerned with challenging every area of life.

Notes

1. Doing theology in the UKKK: towards a redemptive vengeance

1. Audre Lorde, *Sister Outsider: essays and speeches by Audre Lorde* (California, The Crossing Press, 1988), p. 42.
2. From Black Christian Civic Forum promotional flyer.
3. Kathryn Tanner, *The Politics of God: Christian theologies and social justice* (Minneapolis, Fortress Press, 1992), pp. 19ff.
4. Manning Marable, 'Beyond identity politics: towards a liberating theory for multicultural democracy', *Race and Class* 35 (I), 127.
5. Walter Hollenweger, *Pentecostalism: origins and developments worldwide* (Massachusetts, Hendrickson Publishers, 1997), pp. 18–19.
6. Charles Fox Parham in Iain MacRobert, *Black Roots and White Racism in Early Pentecostalism in the USA* (London, Macmillan, 1988).
7. I am suggesting that Seymour developed the doctrine of tongues beyond the theological ideas passed on to him by Charles Fox Parham. It is Parham who is credited with the development of the doctrine, but Seymour made it a socio-political reality at Azusa Street.
8. Roswith Gerloff, *A Plea for British Black Theologies: the Black Church movement in Britain in its Transatlantic cultural and theological interaction*, Vol.1 (Frankfurt, Peter Lang, 1992), p. 102.
9. See also the preface in Michael Eric Dyson, *Between God and Gangsta Rap: bearing witness to Black culture* (Oxford, Oxford University Press, 1996).
10. A. Anderson, 'Pentecostal pneumatology and African power concepts: continuity and change', *Missionalia* 19 (1), April 1990, 65–74.
11. D. J. Nelson, 'For Such a Time as This: The Story of Bishop William

J. Seymour and the Azusa Street Revival', unpublished PhD dissertation, University of Birmingham, May 1981, p. 120.

12. I. Clemmons, 'True Koinonia: Pentecostal hopes and historical realities', *Pneuma* 3 (1), 1981, 46–56.

13. See R. Beckford, *Dread and Pentecostal: a political theology for the Black Church in Britain* (London, SPCK, 2000) pp. 173ff.

14. Hollenweger, *Pentecostalism*, p. 20.

15. Iain MacRobert, *The Black Roots and White Racism of Early Pentecostalism in the USA* (London, Macmillan, 1988), p. 35.

16. See M. Warren, *Seeing Through the Media: a religious view of communications and cultural analysis* (Pennsylvania, Trinity Press, 1997), pp. 48ff.

17. bell hooks, *Outlaw Culture: resisting representation* (London, Routledge, 1994).

18. Fred Hickling, unpublished paper presented at the Black Theology Support Group, 22 March 2000.

19. Frantz Fanon, *Black Skin White Masks* (London, Pluto, 1991), pp. 210ff.

20. Richard D. Burton, *Afro-Creole: power, play and opposition in the Caribbean* (Ithaca, NY, Cornell University Press, 1997), pp. 62–4.

21. E. Lartey, *In Living Colour: an intercultural approach to pastoral care and counselling* (London, Cassell, 1997), p. 47.

22. Henry Louis Gates, *The Signifying Monkey* (New York, Oxford University Press, 1988), p. 74.

23. See Horace Campbell, *Rasta and Resistance: from Marcus Garvey to Walter Rodney* (London, Hansib Publishing Ltd, 1985), p. 23.

24. See Patricia A. Turner, *I Heard it through the Grapevine: rumor in African-American culture* (Los Angeles and London, California University Press, 1993), pp. 202ff.

25. Theophus Smith, *Conjuring Culture: biblical formations of Black America* (Oxford, Oxford University Press, 1994), p. 44.

26. This idea must be credited to my colleague Y. Hutchinson.

27. Robert E. Hood, *Begrimed and Black: Christian traditions on Blacks and Blackness* (Minneapolis, Fortress Press, 1994), pp. 23ff.

28. Burton, *Afro-Creole*, pp. 103ff.

29. The argument that Christ is found in the work/ministry of African women. See Kelly Brown Douglas, *The African Caribbean Christ* (Maryknoll, NY, Orbis, 1994), pp. 107ff.

30. Michelle Wallace, *Invisibility Blues: from pop to theory* (London, Verso, 1994), p. 243.
31. See Hood, *Begrimed and Black*, pp. 103ff.
32. See Beckford, *Dread and Pentecostal*, p. 187.
33. Sir William Macpherson of Cluny, *The Stephen Lawrence Inquiry* (London, The Stationery Office, 1999), Sec. 6.33.
34. Cited in Robert E. Hood, *Must God Remain Greek? Afro-cultures and God-talk* (Minneapolis, Fortress Press, 1990), p. 89.
35. M. Foucault, *The History of Sexuality: an introduction*, Vol. 1, trans. Robert Hurley (New York, Vantage Books, 1990), pp. 95–6.
36. I refer to Hazel Carby's universally acclaimed 80s essay on the sisterhood between Black and White women in England. See Hazel Carby, 'White women listen! Black feminism and the boundaries of sisterhood' in H. S. Mirza (ed.), *Black British Feminism: a reader* (London, Routledge, 1997).
37. *The Voice*, 15 February 1999.
38. See L. A. Decaro, *Malcolm and the Cross: The Nation of Islam, Malcolm X and Christianity* (New York, New York University Press, 1998).
39. Michael Eric Dyson, *I May Not Get There with You: The True Martin Luther King Jr* (New York, Free Press, 1980), p. 6.
40. See Gates, *The Signifying Monkey*, pp. 51–2.
41. Jamaican term for White overseer.

2. God of the rahtid: redemptive vengeance

1. Robert Beckford, *Jesus is Dread: Black theology and Black culture in Britain* (London, DLT, 1998).
2. James Cone, *Black Theology and Black Power* (New York, Harper & Row, 1989), pp. 71ff.
3. Anthony Pinn, *Why Lord? suffering and evil in Black theology* (New York, Continuum, 1995), p. 15.
4. See D. Williams, *Sisters in the Wilderness: the challenge of womanist God talk* (New York, Orbis, 1993), pp. 161ff.
5. See J. Riches, *Jesus and the Transformation of Judaism* (London 1980), pp. 77–111.
6. Stella Orakwue, *Pitch Invaders: the modern Black football revolution* (London, Victor Gollancz, 1998), p. 9.
7. Joe Feagin and Melvin P. Sikes, *Living with Racism: the Black middle-class experience* (Boston, Beacon, 1994).

8. P. H. Collins, *Fighting Words: Black women and the search for justice* (Minneapolis, Minnesota University Press, 1998), p. 38.

9. Tony Sewell, *Black Masculinities and Schooling: how Black boys survive modern schooling* (London, Trentham Books, 1997), pp. 25ff.

10. Sewell, *Black Masculinities*, pp. 101ff.

11. K. Mercer, 'Racism and politics of masculinity' in R. Chapman and J. Rutherford (eds.), *Male Order: unwrapping masculinity* (London, Lawrence & Wishart, 1988).

12. See www.niceup.com/patois.txt.

13. P. H. Collins, *Black Feminist Thought: knowledge, consciousness and the politics of empowerment* (London, Routledge, 1990), pp. 208ff.

14. V. Alexander, 'Breaking Every Fetter'? To What Extent Has the Black Led Church in Britain Developed a Theology of Liberation?' PhD thesis, University of Warwick, 1997. I. MacRobert, 'Black Pentecostalism, its Origins, Functions and Theology', unpublished PhD thesis, University of Birmingham, 1989. R. Gerloff, *A Plea for British Black Theologies: the Black Church movement in Britain in its Transatlantic cultural and theological interaction*, Vol.1 (Frankfurt, Peter Lang, 1992).

15. Howard Clark Kee and Franklin W. Young, *The Living World of the New Testament* (London, Darton, Longman and Todd, 1974), p. 62.

16. James Cone, *Black Theology and Black Power* (San Francisco, Harper & Row Publishers, 1989), p. 123.

17. James Cone, *God of the Oppressed* (San Francisco, Harper Collins, 1975), p. 160.

18. James Cone, *A Black Theology of Liberation*, 2nd edn (Maryknoll, NY, Orbis, 1986), p. 126.

19. Karen Baker-Fletcher and Garth Kasimu Baker-Fletcher, *My Brother, My Sister: womanist and Xodus God-talk* (Maryknoll, NY, Orbis, 1996), p. 284.

20. ibid. p. 290.

21. ibid. p. 293.

22. bell hooks, *Killing Rage: ending racism* (New York, Henry Holt & Company, 1995), p. 16.

23. ibid.

24. Lemn Sissay, *The Fire People: a collection of contemporary Black British poets* (London, Payback Press, 1998).

25. L. K. Johnson, *Tings an Times: selected poems* (Newcastle upon Tyne, Bloodaxe Books, 1997).
26. Fred D'Aguiar, Introduction to L. K. Johnson, *Inglan is a Bitch* (London, Race Today Publications, 1980).
27. B. Wright, 'Dub poet likka mi: an exploration of poetry, power and identity politics in Black Britain' in K. Owusu (ed.), *Black British Culture and Society* (London, Routledge, 1999).
28. 'Organic intellectuals' are intellectuals grounded in working-class culture.
29. Wright, 'Dub poet likka mi'.
30. Cornel West, *Race Matters* (Boston, Beacon Press, 1994), pp. 95–6.
31. Willa Boesak, *God's Wrathful Children: political oppression and Christian ethics* (Michigan, William B. Eerdmans, 1995), pp. 202ff.
32. Miroslav Volf, *Exclusion and Embrace: a theological exploration of identity, otherness and reconciliation* (Atlanta, Abingdon Press, 1996) p. 105.
33. A. D. Callahan, *Embassy of Onesimus: the Letter of Paul to Philemon* (Pennsylvania, Trinity Press, 1997), pp. 61–2.
34. Gustavo Gutiérrez, *Theology of Liberation*, 3rd edn (Maryknoll, NY, Orbis, 1988), p. xxxviii.
35. bell hooks, *All about Love: new visions* (New York, William Morrow & Co. Inc., 1999).

3. Name droppin': redeeming a slave name

1. S. Hall, 'Cultural identity and diaspora' in J. Rutherford (ed.), *Identity, Community Culture and Difference* (London, Sage, 1990), p. 225.
2. See D. Hiro, *Black British, White British: a story of race relations in Britain* (London, Paladin Press, 1992), pp. 21ff.
3. bell hooks, *Art on My Mind: visual politics* (New York, The New Press, 1995), p. 74.
4. Anthony Pinn, *Varieties of African American Religious Experience* (Minneapolis, Fortress Press, 1998), p. 189.
5. J. Cone, *Risk of Faith: the emergence of a Black theology of liberation, 1969–1998* (Boston, Beacon Press, 1999), p. 130.
6. ibid. p. 132.
7. For a full account of the *Zong* massacre see Peter Fryer, *Staying Power: the history of Black people in Britain* (London, Pluto Press, 1984), pp. 127–30.

8. Clive Harris and Winston James (eds.), *Inside Babylon: the Caribbean diaspora in Britain* (London, Verso, 1993), pp. 55ff.
9. Paul Gilroy, *The Black Atlantic: modernity and double consciousness* (London, Verso, 1993).
10. Barry Chevannes, *Rastafari: roots and ideology* (New York, Syracuse University Press, 1994), p. 20.
11. ibid. pp. 22ff.
12. See Earl Riggins, *Dark Symbols, Obscure Signs: God, self and community in the slave mind* (Maryknoll, NY, Orbis, 1993).
13. Noel Erskine, *Decolonising Theology: a Caribbean perspective* (Trenton, NJ, African World Press, 1998), pp. 142ff.
14. J. Lees-Milne, *William Beckford* (London, Century, 1976), p. 1.
15. Timothy Mowle, *William Beckford: composing for Mozart* (London, John Murray, 1998), p. 288.
16. ibid. p. 1.
17. See Stella Dadzie, 'Searching for the invisible woman: slavery and resistance in Jamaica', *Race and Class* 32 (October–December 1990), 21–38.
18. Karen Baker-Fletcher and Garth Kasimu Baker-Fletcher, *My Brother, My Sister: womanist and Xodus God-talk* (Maryknoll, NY, Orbis, 1996), pp. 16ff.
19. A. S. Caglar, 'Hyphenated identities and the limits of culture' in T. Modood and P. Werbner (eds.), *The Politics of Multiculturalism in the New Europe* (London, Zed Books, 1997), pp. 175ff.
20. Kelly Brown Douglas, *Sexuality and the Black Church: a womanist Perspective* (Maryknoll, NY, Orbis, 1999), p. 32.
21. Claire Alexander, *The Art of Being Black* (Oxford, Oxford University Press, 1996), p. 18.
22. M. K. Asante, *Afrocentricity* (Trenton, NJ, African World Press, 1990), p. 101.

4. Miseducation: Lauryn Hill and redemptive vengeance

1. Theophus Smith, *Conjuring Culture: the biblical formations of Black America* (Oxford, Oxford University Press, 1994), pp. 5, 6.
2. A useful definition is found in Jon Michael Spencer, preface to *The Theology of American Popular Music*, a special issue of *Black Sacred Music: a journal of theomusicology* 3 (2), fall 1989.

> A theologically informed discipline . . . a musicological method for theologising about the sacred (the religious/churched), the secular (the theistic unreligious/unchurched), and the profane

(the atheistic/irreligious) – including sacred and nonsacred music functioning as theomusicotherapy in church and community – principally incorporating methods borrowed from anthropology, sociology, psychology, and philosophy.

3. T. Rose, *Black Noise: rap music and Black culture in contemporary America* (New England, Wesleyan University Press, 1994), pp. 21–5.
4. ibid. p. 34.
5. U. Poschardt, *DJ Culture* (London, Quartet Books, 1995), p. 155.
6. M. Holman, *Breaking and the New York City Breakers* (New York 1984), p. 61.
7. Nelson George, 'Hip-hop's founding fathers', *The Source* 11/1993, 47.
8. Stuart Hall, 'What is the "Black" in Black Popular Culture' in G. Dent, *Black Popular Culture* (Seattle, Bay Press, 1994), p. 27.
9. Nelson George, *Hip-Hop America* (New York, Viking Penguin, 1988), p. 17.
10. Poschardt, *DJ Culture*, pp. 167–74.
11. George, *Hip-Hop America*, p. 18.
12. Poschardt, *DJ Culture*, p. 176.
13. From WWW.International Zulu Nation.
14. Paul Gilroy, *The Black Atlantic: modernity and double consciousness* (London, Verso, 1994), pp. 103–4.
15. Rose, *Black Noise*, p. 39.
16. Garth Baker-Fletcher, *Xodus: an African American male journey* (Minneapolis, Fortress Press, 1996), pp. 137–8.
17. See Todd Boyd, *Am I Black Enough for You? popular culture from the hood and beyond* (Bloomington, IN, Indiana University Press, 1997), p. 61.
18. Baker-Fletcher, *Xodus*, p. 143.
19. Anthony Pinn, *Why Lord? suffering and evil in Black theology* (New York, Continuum, 1995), p. 143.
20. Michael Eric Dyson, *Reflecting Black: African American cultural criticism* (Minneapolis, University of Minnesota Press, 1993), pp. 276ff.
21. Dyson, *Reflecting Black*, p. 227.
22. See Michael Eric Dyson, *Between God and Gangsta Rap: bearing witness to Black culture* (Oxford, Oxford University Press, 1996), pp. 165–77.
23. Cornel West, 'The new cultural politics of difference' in Russell

Furgerson, Martha Gever, Trinh T. Minh-ha and Cornel West (eds.), *Out There: marginalization and contemporary cultures* (New York and Cambridge, MA, The New Museum of Contemporary Art and MIT Press, 1990), pp. 19–20.

24. Baker-Fletcher, *Xodus*, pp. 147–9.
25. Victor Anderson, *Beyond Ontological Blackness* (New York, Continuum, 1995), pp. 20–32.
26. K. Eshun, *More Brilliant than the Sun: adventures in sonic fiction* (London, Quartet Books, 1998), p. 5.
27. ibid. p. 37.
28. ibid. p. 14.
29. ibid. p. 4.
30. ibid.
31. Paul Gilroy, *Small Acts: thoughts on the politics of Black cultures* (London, Serpent's Tail, 1993), p. 254.
32. Eshun, *More Brilliant than the Sun*, p. 41.
33. ibid. p. 22.
34. M. Lieb, *Children of Ezekiel: aliens, UFOS, the crisis of race, and the advent of end time* (Durham and London, Duke University Press, 1999).
35. Taken from the sleeve of 4 Hero's album, *Two Pages* (London, Mercury Records, 1998).
36. Kelly Brown Douglas, 'God is as Christ does: towards a womanist theology', *Journal of Religious Thought* 1 (1988), 7–17.
37. Stephen Howe, *Afrocentrism: mythical past and imagined homes* (London, Verso, 1998), p. 1.
38. 'Final Hour', *The Miseducation of Lauryn Hill* (Ruff House Records, 1988).
39. See Barry Chevanees, *Rastafari: roots and ideology* (New York, Syracuse University Press, 1994), p. 82.
40. Cheryl Kirk-Duggan, *Exorcising Evil: a womanist perspective on the spirituals* (Maryknoll, NY, Orbis, 1997), p. 143.
41. Cornel West, *Race Matters* (Boston, Beacon Press, 1994), pp. 35ff.
42. Quoted in R. McAfee-Brown, *Religion and Violence*, 2nd edn (Philadelphia, Westminster Press, 1987), p. xxii.
43. Cornel West, 'Learning to talk of race' in R. Gooding-Williams (ed.), *Reading Rodney King, Reading Urban Uprising* (New York, Routledge, 1993), pp. 256–7.
44. Paul Gilroy, *Against Race: imagining political culture beyond the*

colour line (Cambridge, MA, The Belknap Press of Harvard University Press, 2000), pp. 196–7.

5. *Redeeming the hustler (Part 1): Black male offenders and redemptive vengeance*

1. J. Lea and J. Young, *What Is to be Done about Law and Order?* 2nd edn (London, Pluto Press, 1993).
2. Stephen Moore, *Investigating Crime and Deviance* (London, Collins Educational, 1996), pp. 245ff.
3. J. Cone, *God of the Oppressed* (San Francisco; Harper Collins, 1975), p. 75.
4. Delores Williams, *Sisters in the Wilderness: the challenge of womanist God-talk* (Maryknoll, NY, Orbis, 1993), pp. 167–9.
5. James W. Messerschmidt, *Crime and Structured Action: gender, race, class and crime in the making* (London, Sage, 1997), p. 53.
6. Patricia Hill Collins, *Black Feminist Thought: knowledge, consciousness and the politics of empowerment* (London, Routledge, 1990), pp. 212–14.
7. T. Smith, *Conjuring Culture: biblical formations of Black America* (Oxford, Oxford University Press, 1994), pp. 5–6.
8. Eugene Franklin Wong, *On Visual Media Racism: Asians in American motion pictures* (New York, Garland, 1978).
9. Robyn Wiegman, 'Race, ethnicity and film' in John Hill and Pamela Church Gibson (eds.), *The Oxford Guide to Film Studies* (Oxford, Oxford University Press, 1999), p. 158.
10. ibid. p. 165.

Acknowledgements

Bass Culture
Words & Music by Linton Kwesi Johnson
© Copyright 1980 L-K-J Music Publisher Ltd
Universal/Island Music Limited, 77 Fulham Palace Road,
London W6.
Used by permission of Music Sales Ltd
All Rights Reserved. International Copyright Secured

Reality Poem
Words & Music by Linton Kwesi Johnson
© Copyright 1978 L-K-J Music Publisher Ltd
LKJ Music Publisher Ltd/Universal/Island Music Limited, 77 Fulham
Palace Road, London W6.
Used by permission of Music Sales Ltd
All Rights Reserved. International Copyright Secured

Fite Dem Back
Words & Music by Linton Kwesi Johnson
© Copyright 1979 L-K-J Music Publisher Ltd
LKJ Music Publisher Ltd/Universal/Island Music Limited, 77 Fulham
Palace Road, London W6.
Used by permission of Music Sales Ltd
All Rights Reserved. International Copyright Secured

Liesense Fi Kill
Words & Music by Linton Kwesi Johnson
© Copyright 1980 L-K-J Music Publisher Ltd
LKJ Music Publisher Ltd/Universal/Island Music Limited, 77 Fulham
Palace Road, London W6.
Used by permission of Music Sales Ltd
All Rights Reserved. International Copyright Secured